A

SHORT HISTORY

OF THE

EGYPTIAN OBELISKS.

BY

W. R. COOPER, F.R.A.S., M.R.A.S.,

Secretary to the Society of Biblical Archæology.

WITH TRANSLATIONS OF MANY OF THE HIEROGLYPHIC INSCRIPTIONS;
CHIEFLY BY

M. FRANÇOIS CHABAS.

ISBN: 978-1-63923-980-1

Printed: March 2023

Published and Distributed By:
Lushena Books
607 Country Club Drive, Unit E
Bensenville, IL 60106
www.lushenabks.com

ISBN: 978-1-63923-980-1

TO

SIR WILLIAM W. BURTON, Knt.,

LATE JUDGE
OF H.M. SUPREME COURT, MADRAS.

Dear Sir,

Please to accept the dedication to yourself of this little Book, the completion of which has brought back to my mind many pleasant memories; not the least of which are those of your hospitality to me at Cheltenham in 1874, and constant friendship since.

Yours faithfully,

W. R. Cooper

Ventnor, *October* 1, 1877.

PREFACE.

IN the following pages I have endeavoured to arrange, in something like consecutive order, all that is definitely known concerning the History of the Egyptian Obelisks generally; and more particularly of those now standing. To do this it has been necessary to compare the accounts of many writers, and the measurements of various authors, but the result of such a comparison is far from satisfactory; in truth there is very little agreement between them; and there are several statements which cannot be reconciled with each other. Under these difficulties, I have had to rely chiefly upon the measurements of Bonomi, he being professionally a sculptor as well as an Egyptologist, and, therefore, possessing a double guarantee against liability to errors of detail. With regard to the identifications of the obelisks mentioned by Pliny with those now standing in Rome, it is hardly possible to be quite certain as to any special monument, except perhaps the Obelisk of the Circus Maximus. The original text of Pliny is very vague, and the judgment of Zoega is not wholly to be depended upon. Fortunately these contrarieties do not affect the chief thing in connection with the obelisk to which importance is to be attached: namely, the interpretation of their hieroglyphics, since these latter enable us now to re-construct a history of the monarchs by whom they were erected, from their own contemporaneous records. And here let me add, that I trust that the impetus now given to Egyptian archæology by the splendid gift of the Obelisk of London by Prof. Erasmus Wilson, will not be allowed to dissipate itself after a few months' excitement; but that it will induce many of my readers to study for themselves the language of the Egyptians, which has now become accessible to all students by the Grammar of P. le Page Renouf, and the text books of Dr. Birch, the father of English Egyptology.

I have now to express my sincere thanks to M. François Chabas, for his very valuable aid in freely translating for me the inscriptions upon six of the principal obelisks; to Prof. Erasmus Wilson, who while himself engaged on a similar work, has with singular liberality of sentiment assisted me in my own; to Mr. Hodder Westropp for the loan of many books of reference; and to Dr. Sinclair Coghill, Mr. Westropp of Eglinton, the Rev. Clement Hue, of St. Lawrence, Prof. Monier Williams, and Mr. S. M. Drach, for many literary kindnesses in connection with this work.

W. R. COOPER.

VENTNOR,
      October 1, 1877.

CONTENTS.

A SHORT HISTORY OF

THE EGYPTIAN OBELISKS.

CHAPTER I.

Characteristics of an Obelisk.

OF all the monuments of Egypt the most striking and the most characteristic are the Obelisk and the Pyramid; both of them solar emblems: the one significant of the rising, and the other of the setting sun; and both alike dating from that pre-historic period of civilization[1] which was in perfection ere the Father of the Faithful had descended from Ur of the Chaldees, or the Turanian races of India were oppressed by their Aryan brethren.

For so long a succession of centuries has the Obelisk been admired and copied in the various cities of Africa, Asia, and Europe; Alexandria, Constantinople, and Rome, that the original peculiarities of the structure itself have been occasionally lost sight of: and any single vertical monument that could not be exactly described as a column, has been set down as an obelisk. Hence there is still in popular acceptance some inaccuracy as to the exact form that an

[1] Pierret, *Dict. Arch. Egyptienne,* "Obelisque," who cites a reference to a pyramid and an obelisk in the "Funereal Inscription of a Priest of the Pyramid Ashet," in the time of the fifth dynasty.

obelisk should assume: and it becomes necessary at once to define what an obelisk is, and what it is not as to external form, before we proceed to examine the intention of its symbolism. An obelisk, or *tekhen*, to give it its Egyptian name, then, is a monument composed of a single quadrangular upright stone, having its four faces inclined towards each other ; and in section, all its angles, right angles, and all its sides parallel to each other ; its height is not less than that of ten diameters, taken at the base; and its apex is abruptly terminated by a small pyramidion, whose faces are inclined at about an angle of sixty degrees. The obelisk is generally supported upon a quadrangular base, the height of which is approximately that of a cube and a half, and which is also, like the obelisk, composed of a single stone, this base is further supported by two broad and deep steps. It is not necessary that the four sides of either obelisk or base[1] have in section the same width, provided that each opposite side is exactly equal; but it is necessary that all the lines of the monument be right lines ; and that it should have no more than four sides. A polygonal, or a cylindrical monolith is not an obelisk ; on the other hand, obelisks may be either inscribed or uninscribed; but the ornamentation is never in relief, other than the low sunken relief used in Egyptian art, and known as *incavo relievo;* and the inscription is always vertical with the lines of the monument, and not horizontal. It must be added, also, that *entasis*, or that slight curvature of all long lines, which is so marked a feature in classic architecture, is wholly foreign to the design of an obelisk in the best period of Pharaohnic art.[2]

[1] The faces of the Flaminian obelisk as drawn by Bonomi are not equal: see Tomlinson on "The Flaminian Obelisk," *Trans. Roy. Soc. Lit.*, Vol. I., p. 176. New Series.

[2] The obelisks of Luxor, of which the one now at Paris is an example, have certainly a convexity or *entasis* on the inner *faces* only; that is an exception to the general rule.

The dimensions of obelisks vary greatly: those of the earlier period being generally the largest, and the simplest in execution. The loftiest now in existence is that which adorns the court of the church of St. John Lateran, at Rome,[1] where it stands a monument, first of the majesty of Thothmes III., by whom it was designed; afterwards of the power of Constantine the Great, who removed it sixteen hundred years later from Heliopolis to Alexandria; and lastly of his successor Constantius who re-erected it in the Circus Maximus of Imperial Rome. The smallest obelisks are the beautiful red granite couple which are now in the Egyptian saloon of the Florentine Museum, and which are respectively seven feet, and five feet ten inches in height. The mutilated and summitless fragments in the British Museum, though now eight feet high, were indisputably loftier when terminated by their original apexes.

The material of which the obelisk was composed was generally a granite, or hard sandstone, capable of being well cut and of taking a high polish. For symbolical reasons which will be hereafter described, the red granite of Syene was chiefly employed: twenty-seven out of the forty-two obelisks now known to exist being wrought' in that imperishable material; the pyramidion at the summit was, when its faces were not sculptured with votive vignettes, covered with a cap of either bronze or gold: the obelisks of Hatasu at Karnak being described in the hieroglyphic texts as thus completed in that costly metal, while the bronze cap of the obelisk at Heliopolis remained entire till the middle ages, having reached the notice of the eminent physician and historian Abd-el-lateef who flourished circa 1300. No obelisks however now

[1] In this I follow the measurements given by Bonomi, the best writer on the subject of obelisks. Pierret however cites the obelisk of Hatasu at Karnak as being the loftiest known: it being 33 metres high; while that of St. John Lateran is, according to the same authority, 32 only.

remain thus completed, the avarice of poverty or the rapacity of war having stripped from these, as well as the other monuments of Egypt, every fragment of exposed metal either to furnish gold for the extortions of the Turkish governors, or swords or guns for the defence, more often the destruction, of the Fellaheen.

CHAPTER II.

The Symbolism of the Obelisk.

IN its original conception, the religion of Egypt was a pure monotheism, a monotheism of the most refined character, which admitted even to the last no *portraiture* of the Supreme Being, but adored him in his visible manifestations, and symbolised his character by allegorical representations founded upon a human form. The distinction between portraiture and symbolic representation must be strictly recollected by the student of Egyptian theology, who is accustomed to look upon a multitude of gods, of a more or less animal nature, as characteristic of the worship of the banks of the Nile. This mistake, as old as the time of the Grecian historians, aroused the keenest notes of the satirical lyre of Juvenal,' and has perpetuated the most contemptuous ridicule in the writings of the early Fathers of the Christian church; but though not immediately apparent, the differentiation between portraiture and symbolic statuary is perfectly real and natural, and, if anything, modern religious art carries out the more faulty conception of the two. When a modern worshipper looks upon the reverend furrowed features and grey beard of the first person of the Trinity in the accepted *chefs d'œuvres* of

' *Satire*, XV., Lines 1-9.

Catholic art, or when he implores pity at the feet of the languid-eyed long-haired Madonna of Italian sculpture, he unconsciously regards the divine personage so represented, as so looking ; and Christian iconography has accepted a perfectly well-defined ideal likeness of every person in the Godhead.[1] Not so the Egyptian devotee: he never attributed to Ra or Anubis the actual possession of a human body with either the beak of a hawk, or the snout of a jackal; a cow-headed Isis or a snake-headed Horus, though both common enough in the temple statuary, was regarded simply as an allegorical conception, a sculptured metaphor to convey to the mind's eye the attributes of a being, who was himself inconceivable and indescribable. In the higher mysteries of the sacred books, the Great Supreme was spoken of as the creator and controller of all the gods, who were but his various manifestations; while the Sun itself, that mysterious luminary upon whose beneficent beams all human or vegetable life depended, was regarded as his clearest symbol, and as partaking in some degree of the divine essence; and it was therefore worshipped throughout Egypt with a universal veneration.

Upon the position of the sun, then, its gradual rise from the eastern horizon, its glorious enthronization in the mid-day firmament, and its gentle decline behind the mountains of the west, from thence to traverse during the twelve hours of night the mysterious regions of the Underworld: upon its course along the heavens, and its station in all these positions, the theology of Egypt was based. Based theoretically on a spiritual, it became practically a solar, worship : the sun being venerated under its two chief deifications, Ra the rising and mid-day sun, to whose cultus the obelisk was appropriated, and Tum the setting or midnight sun, the emblem of whose

[1] See Didron's *Christian Iconography*.

influence was the pyramid.   In Ra, according to the solar litanies, were combined all the attributes of power and wisdom; the source of life and the springs of health were his; every characteristic quality of each of the multiform lesser deities of Egypt he possessed in full perfection, and the noblest and most exalted language was used to describe his nature and offices.   The soul of man, which emanated originally from his own essence, rose from the pre-existent eternity with him, and descended for a time into the shades of the Underworld, there still to venerate its maker, and again to arise purified and justified till it was eventually reabsorbed into the solar orb from which it was first emitted.   The Litany of Ra, one of the most famous of the sacred liturgies of the Egyptians, declares the deity to be "An Eternal Essence;" "Self Created;" "*The* Supreme Power;" "The Original;" "The Creator of his own Members," that is of his own manifestations, the active life of all things; "The Father of the Eternal Son," *i.e.*, of Horus who performed in Egyptian mythology the part of a justifier and a redeemer of the believers in Ra; "The Spirit of Space filling all things;" "The Invisible;" "The Ruler of Heaven and Hell;" "The Revealer of Secrets;" "The Cause of both Light and Darkness;" "The Dweller in Inapproachable Darkness;" "The Breath of all Souls;" "The Cause of all that is;" and "The Most Mysterious God;"[1] in fine, all the deities and all things that exist were but manifestations of himself; nature was reduced to a spiritual pantheism. As the powerful rays of the sun were often suddenly fatal, so the attribute of wrath was ascribed to Ra; but inasmuch as he was too remote and too sublime to experience a personal anger, his vengeful attributes were personified in Shu, the lion-headed god of forces, and Tcfnut, the lion-headed goddess of vengeance. The hawk, that noble bird which in Egypt soared

' See for this in detail *The Myth of Ra*, by the author of this work, p. 26, 28.

highest of all flying creatures, was sacred to the sun ; the bull amongst animals, because he was both the strongest, and because his powers of generation were believed to be instantaneous, was honoured as his representative, as he is to this day in Southern India for nearly the same reason. The supreme, as the sun, reigned dominant, sole and eternal in Egyptian mythology ; his glory might indeed be manifested in another deity but it could not be shared by it, inasmuch as in certain operations the sun, as Ra, was believed to assume a lower position in the relation which one attribute bore to the other, and therefore was ranked occasionally as one of the secondary deities ; it was merely an official not a spiritual subordination: Ra still remained all in all, whether he were called Ra-Tum, Amen-Ra (the hidden), Ra-Harmakhu (the sun in the horizon), Horus-Ra, the mediatory god, or Kheper-Ra, the creator; in the last character being represented by the sacred scarabeus holding the cosmic ball between his front legs.[1]

Of this all-powerful deity the obelisk was considered to be the most technical symbol: inasmuch as its sharply defined lines and narrow proportions, conjoined with its immense height, gave no imperfect representation of a pencil or ray of light, such as would often be seen darting vertically downwards through the crevices of the gathering clouds. For this reason also, granite, as being the most durable material, was generally chosen, that the least destructible stone might represent the eternal sun ; and the colour red, was likewise selected as analogous to the hue of the disk of the sun, when viewed across the sands of the Lybian desert. There was also a further reason why the obelisk was

---

[1] The scarabeus, *Ateuchis Sacer,* was regarded as an emblem of the sun, because it was in the habit of laying its eggs in a ball of dung or clay, which it kept rolling before it till they were vivified by the direct heat of the sun. See also Woodwrooffe's *Monograph on the Scarabeus.*

dedicated to the sun as the creator, but that reason is one which can only be here alluded to, as affording one of the earliest indications of a form of nature worship which has led to the most painful and objectionable excesses.'

As the king while living was theologically regarded as both a son of Ra, and also by an hypostasis, Ra himself, it followed as a corollary that the inscriptions on the obelisk were generally honorific of the sovereign by whom it was erected, and that they conveyed more the declarations of Ra to the monarch than any direct homage of the Pharaoh to the god. Hence the very little historical value of the obelisk texts in general; few of them were dated; they consisted chiefly of the same monotonous list of official epithets and magniloquent titles, with the so-called banner name, or Horus title of the sovereign, at the top, a title which he assumed as the personation of Horus-Ra himself; and on the sides of the pyramidion, or sometimes at the lower portion of the monument, a vignette, representing either the king standing and making an offering to Amen-Ra, or else kneeling at the feet of the god, who was figured as investing him with the sacred crown of the double kingdom, and commissioning him to conquer all nations, and to take the spoils of all lands.

As the execution of an obelisk was a work of considerable time, and as it was always sculptured after it had been permanently placed in position; it not unfrequently happened, as will be hereafter shown in the cases of the Luxor and Lateran obelisks, that a

---

' Pierret, *Dict. Arch. Egypt.*, "Obelisque." There is, however, no reason to believe that at the early period of Egyptian history, or indeed till after the Greek invasion under the Psammetichi, there was any obscenity either of thought or action connected with the symbolical worship of the obelisk. The nature of this worship is beyond dispute, for in the Museum of the Louvre there is a mummied phallus preserved in an upright wooden case shaped like an obelisk, and honoured as a symbol of Amen the generator.

monument erected by one Pharaoh has been completed by another; and where the centre line of inscription has been finished by the original dedicator, his son or successor has subsequently added parallel columns setting forth his own glory; and in one or two examples the second appropriator has had the meanness to attempt to erase the cartouch of his preceder and to substitute his own, an attempt that has not in any case been successful, an attempt besides of the meanest character, and according to the rules of Egyptian mythology of the basest and most cruel nature; as by the obliteration of the name of an individual from his stele or monument, the spiritual life of that person was itself imperilled. Of this disgraceful conduct, one of the greatest Pharaohs of Egypt, Thothmes III., had the pettyness to be guilty, by the defacement of the name of his great sister queen Hatasu, at Deir-el-bahri; a meanness rendered only the more glaringly apparent, by the inability of the forger to erase or alter the personal pronouns in the whole of the long dedications which would not grammatically agree with the titles and cartouch of Thothmes.[1]

In concluding this chapter, it remains but to be stated that a still more serious defacement of the Egyptian monuments, and obelisks in particular, took place upon two occasions, when for religious motives which are not quite apparent at this lapse of time, the figure of the god Set was hammered out wherever it occurred in a royal cartouch, and that of Ra substituted for it. At another period also the *name* as well as the figure of Amen suffered the like erasement, and there is evidence that these alterations must have been by order of a very powerful change of religious feeling: for the objectionable names were

---

[1] This point has been well brought out in Miss Keary's admirable little *History of Egypt from the Monuments.*

obliterated and the others reinscribed on the most inaccessible portions of the temples, as well as on the bases of the votive statues. And in the instance of the obelisk of the Lateran, a scaffolding must have been erected for the sole purpose of chiselling out a portion of a few small cartouches at the very summit of the monolith : cartouches which were almost invisible from the ground, at the height at which they were carved.[1]

CHAPTER III.

Relations of the Obelisk and the Pyramid.

THE first mention of the obelisk, or *tekhen*, occurs in connection with the pyramid: and both are alike designated sacred monuments on the funeral stele of the early empire, and also were undeniably devoted to the worship of the sun ; occasionally the obelisk was represented as surmounting a pyramid, a position which it has never actually been found to occupy. The fundamental idea of the obelisk was doubtless that of light and creation, but towards the period of the XXIInd dynasty, the syllabic value of stability was attached to it, a characteristic hitherto only symbolised by the Nilometer, or *tat* 𓊽, and the

---

[1] Pierret, *Dict. Arch. Egypt.*, "Martelage des Cartouches." The monuments of the usurping kings of the XIIIth and subsequent dynasties, have been defaced and appropriated by the Pharaohs of the XVIIIth or XIXth. Atefnuter Ai, of the XVIIIth dynasty, had his name erased by his successors on account of his illegitimacy; Amenhotep IV., on account of his heresy in the proscription of the worship of Amen for that of Aten **Ra** ; and Shabaka the Ethiopian, because he was an usurper. The chief defacers of the monuments of their predecessors were the famous monarchs Thothmes III. and Rameses II., both actuated apparently by motives of jealousy.

monument was then termed *Men*, which was a portion of the divine name of the deity Amen-Ra, to whom it was generally dedicated.[1] These ideas came naturally: as the expression of Egyptian mythology Amen-Ra, or Ra as the generator could be properly represented as "Lord of Obelisks," implying lord of stability in the heavenly world, as Osiris was called "Lord of Tattu," and was represented by two *tats*, emblems of his stability as judge of the dead, and lord of the lower world; while the pyramid *ab mer* symbolised the midnight or subterranean sun. Hence arose both the connection and the differentiation between the two classes of votivi, a differentiation not sufficiently regarded, but which was in itself highly significant. These differences deserve numerical notice here: 1. The obelisks of Egypt are all situated on the eastern side of the Nile, that being the district of the rising sun,[2] while all the pyramids are located on the western bank of the river, the land of the sun setting; located amidst rock cut cemeteries, and the tumuli of the undistinguished dead of many generations. 2. The obelisk was invariably a monolith, and stood upon a base either cubiform, or of one or two steps or gradines. The pyramids were always composed of several courses of stone, even where the position of the ground allowed of their being like the sphynx cut out of the natural rock. 3. Obelisks were almost invariably erected in pairs, fronting the chief pylons of the greater temples; they preserved a symmetrical relation to each other; and they were surrounded by colonnades and aediculi, or smaller temples, dedicated to the lesser deities, or to the king as himself a deity. On the other hand, with the sole exception of the so-called pyramids of Mœris or

[1] Pierret, *Dict.*, p. 383.
[2] Bonomi on "Obelisks," *Trans. Roy. Soc. Lit.*, Vol. I., Second Series, p. 168.

Amenemha III.,[1] of which no remains now exist, the pyramids were always though congregated in groups, yet arranged independently of each other ; and the principle of duplication was not followed in their distribution. 4. The obelisks were generally inscribed, and those which remain without an inscription were evidently prepared to receive one. Their intention was to exalt the glory of the living monarch, the son of the sun, or Ra. The pyramids have no external inscription (the testimony of Herodotus notwithstanding) ;[2] whatever hieroglyphics there were, were reserved for the sepulchral coffin, and the chamber in which it was deposited. The inscription in a pyramid had reference to the dead, the Osiride Pharaoh, and not to the reigning sovereign. 5. The obelisks were in many cases tipped with a metal covering; the pyramids were on the other hand covered by a casing of polished stones, which several of them still retain in a more or less perfect condition, a fate which has not befallen the brasen summits of the more slender monuments. 6. Many of the obelisks of Egypt occupy no longer, even in their own country, their original situation: those of Alexandria were removed from On to

---

[1] The pyramids of king Mœris were said to have been placed in the centre of the great reservoir or lake, which that monarch caused to be excavated to preserve the waters of the Nile against a time of drought. Upon the summit of each pyramid was erected a statue of the monarch and his wife respectively. The lake has been calculated to have covered an area of 10,000,000 metres, and a portion of it still remains, and forms the great swamps called the Birket Kerun. Mœris has been identified with Amenemha III., one of the greatest monarchs of the XIIth dynasty, and the probable founder of the Labyrinth; but of his two pyramids nothing now is to be found.

[2] The inscription described by Herodotus, *Euterpe*, 124, as giving an account of the cost of the food of the workmen, which in vegetables and garlic amount to 1000 talents of silver, was probably written on a tablet outside the great pyramid, if indeed it was not a confused rendering of the usual formula on the funeral stele, "Give ye thousands of loaves, fruit, onions, etc., for the justified," after which followed the name and titles of the deceased.

Alexandria, and that of Heliopolis was probably re-erected in a later period than that of the monarch whose name it bears. Twelve, if not more obelisks, were carried off to Italy by the Romans, two were transported to Nineveh by Assurbanipal on the establishment of the Dodecarchy, and these two it is to be regretted have not yet been found, probably they still remain under the *debris* of the city of Assur. On the other hand, not one of the pyramids has been removed from its place, several have been destroyed, and many mutilated, but though the Romans imitated the work of the Egyptians in the pyramid of Caius Cestius, and probably other funereal monuments also, they never attempted to carry and re-erect any of the smaller pyramids, which they might easily have done. 7. Lastly, it may be observed that the name of the erecters of the obelisks are mostly all known to us, while those of the founders of the lesser pyramids are either lost or else are difficult to identify. The stelæ of the priests of many of the deified pyramid builders of the Vth dynasty remain, but the identical structures to which they were attached cannot now be verified, they are among the many historical data which time, more revengeful even than ambition, has erased from the tablets of archæology.

It is in itself a remarkable peculiarity of everything connected with the worship of the Ancient Egyptians, that it had its rise long prior to the genesis of Classic history; that it existed in full power contemporaneously with the theologies of India, Greece, Etruria, and Rome, and that it, overlapping Christianity itself, only ceased to become venerated when all material worship had been swept away; neither the philosophy of Plato, nor the atheism of Cicero could influence beyond a certain limit the term of the Egyptian mythology; it still awed the mixed multitudes in Alexandria under the sway of the Cæsars,

as it had done the ancient Egyptians, "the pure men,"
as they called themselves in the time of Menes and
Athothes ; the tributes of distant countries were still
brought by the Ptolemies to the shrine of Tum,
as they had been a thousand years before by
Rameses III.,' and Alexander and Darius paid
homage to Amen-Ra in the temple which his Egyptian votaries had erected to his glory, when the Greeks
were a Nomadic herd, and the Persians unknown
barbarians.

The most ancient of all the existing obelisks, if
we except a small *model*, one discovered by Lepsius
in a tomb of the VIIth dynasty,² is that of Usirtesen
I., of the XIIth dynasty, circa 3064 B.C. ;³ and the
most recent that of Domitian, now in the Piazza
Navona at Rome,⁴ A.D. 81. Thus the Egyptian faith,
as attested by the obelisks alone, covered a space
of more than 3100 years, not including the long
prior period occupied by the first twelve dynasties.
In all that long stretch of time the obelisk was a
sacred monument; was the emblem at once of the
vivifying power of the sun, and of the divine nature
of the king ; a witness for the "right divine to govern

¹ See "Great Harris Papyrus of Rameses III.," in Records *of the Past*,
Vols. III. and V.

² "A few days ago, we found a small obelisk erect, in its original
position, in a tomb (near the pyramids) from the commencement of the
VIIth dynasty. It is only a few feet high, but in good preservation, and
with the name of the occupant of the tomb inscribed upon it. This form
of monument, which is first conspicuous in the new monarchy, is thus
removed several dynasties further back in the old monarchy, even than
the obelisk of Heliopolis." Lepsius, *Letters from Egypt.*

³ According to Lenormant's list in his *Ancient History of the East.* The
dates given by Marriette Bey are still higher, and seem to be fairly well
substantiated.

⁴ Parker, *The Obelisks of Rome*, Plate IV. The translation of this
obelisk, as there given, is certainly open to criticism, "The man god
Horus, the son of the woman Isis," is certainly a Christianly orthodox
method of reading a very usual phrase on the Egyptian monuments.

wrong"[1] for thirty-one centuries at least. There does not exist in any of the capitals of Europe, and perhaps not even in the more ancient cities of Hindustan, a class of objects which have received un-interrupted veneration for as long a time; or which can show as unbroken a succession of religious dedications.[2]

CHAPTER IV.

The Vicissitudes of Obelisks.

WITH but few exceptions, the pyramids, and the sphynx, all the early monuments of Egypt, were twice overthrown: once at the close of the VIth dynasty by a revolution of which absolutely nothing is known, and once again at the close of the XIIth dynasty, by that terrible political revolution which is generally known by the name of the Hykshos invasion; a revolution, the history of which is still obscure, and its origin and termination are still moot points in archæology.

The dynasty of the Usirtesens, and Amenemhas, had been one of domestic peace and national glory. Great roads had been levelled, a huge reservoir constructed to receive the overflow of the waters of the Nile, and to preserve it for a time of drought. New temples had been formed, new cities established, and the capital cities Thebes, Memphis, and Heliopolis, enlarged. Thebes in particular, then a little Southern city, was selected by Usirtesen as a capital, and prepared in part by the foundation of a temple to Amen-

---

[1] Defoe, *Jure Divino.*

[2] The *Bo* trees of Budha, if they really exist, and which would therefore date back to the sixth century B.C., are the nearest sacred objects of an equal antiquity.

Ra, for the great position it afterwards assumed in Egyptian history : the nucleus of the subsequently unrivalled palaces of Karnak. A mercantile intercourse with the Semitic nations, conterminous with the northern and eastern borders of Egypt, had encouraged already the copper and turquoise miners of the Wady Magara ; the Sinaitic peninsula sent its produce to Heliopolis, and the Lybian nations were placed in alliance with the Egyptians ; the chief officers of the court were more or less connected with the royal family, and thus their feudal fidelity was secured ; the priesthood, by instinct but not by caste hereditary, was confined to a few great and wealthy families, and was apparently satisfied with its share. All the external signs of the kingdom indicated a substantial and an increasing prosperity; but within a few years came a reversal, so sad, and so sudden, that it formed a new epoch in the native history, and still remains to us, as it did to the Pharaohs themselves, almost inexplicable in its occurrence.

Where all is conjecture, except the facts upon which the conjectures are based, it is quite legitimate to reason from an hypothesis, and the hypothesis which would account for the success of the Shashu or Hykshos invasion assumes, that the political strength of Egypt had become weakened by the establishment of the new Ethiopic capital of Thebes, by the monarchs of the XIIth dynasty; certain it is, that another dynasty of Egyptian monarchs was reigning at Memphis in lower Egypt, which at the first appears to have been contemporaneous with the XIIth.; this dynasty, indifferently called the XIIIth or XIVth, there is some confusion as to its proper sequence, consisted of about thirty or forty Pharaohs, who were alternately named Sebek-hotep, " Peace of Sebek," [1] and Nefer-hotep, or "Good peace." [2] The

---

[1] The crocodile-headed deity, worshipped at Koum Onebos.

[2] One of the names of the god Khonso, the fire deity, and a kind of demiurgus.

mining stations near Sinai were abandoned; for a divided country no longer could spare an army potent enough to maintain them against the incursions of the neighbouring Arabs; and somewhere about B.C. 2398, the various Nomadic tribes of southern Palestine, led by the warlike Shashu Arabs, and commanded by their respective chieftains or *haq*, crossed the eastern frontier, and invaded the enfeebled country,[1] carrying with them a dualistic theology; and introducing the sole worship of the god Set or Sutekh, an ass-headed deity, who was already considered as one of the minor Egyptian divinities. City by city the lower country fell into the possession of the Hykshos, and those members of the royal family who were sufficiently secured in upper Egypt to maintain their local towns, were reduced to the rank of tributary monarchs. With the religious fury of all invaders, every temple was destroyed by their armies, every monument destroyed or overthrown by their slaves, scarcely a vestige of the architectural splendour of the early dynasties was suffered to remain; and it is believed that the obelisk of Heliopolis was also thrown down and buried in the sand, at the same time that the original temple was destroyed. This terrible rule of the Hykshos, or Shepherd Kings, prevailed for nearly five hundred years, and it rendered the name and occupation of a shepherd ever afterwards odious to an Egyptian. But towards the close of the Shepherd dynasty, the conquerors had become more familiar with the conquered, and had assimilated their arts to those of the natives. In the reign of Apophis, the last of the Hykshos sovereigns, and the probable Pharaoh of Joseph,[2] a complete renaissance of Egyptian art was introduced, and the suppressed religion again manifested a tendency to become powerful. The reconciliation of

[1] Birch, *Rede Lecture*, 1876, p. 23.

[2] This is the view now taken by most of the leading Egyptologists, and accepted by Canon Cook in the *Speaker's Bible*.

the Hykshos came however too late, and one of the
descendants of the Theban Pharaohs, Kames, raised
an army and defeated the now degenerate invaders,
and compelled them to submit to an Egyptian supre-
macy, or to be expelled across the frontier into the arid
deserts from whence they came. Then commenced the
glorious reconstruction of the country. Again were the
temples rebuilt on an enlarged plan, and dedicated to
their wonted deities ; again were obelisks erected, and
cities refounded, and as the aim of the conquerors had
been to obliterate every vestige of the Egyptian art
and faith, so in turn was all that had been instituted
by themselves destroyed, except the worship of Set
or Sutekh, who was relegated to his former position
as an Egyptian local god, and, in the XIXth dynasty
even made the special patron of the Ramesside kings.
Again were temples re-erected, but there can, however, be no doubt that owing chiefly to their slender-
ness, all the earlier obelisks were destroyed, except
those of Usirtesen I.; and indeed that at Biggeg[1] probably remains where it was thrown down, and broken
by the Hykshos.

The next vicissitude to which the obelisks of Egypt
were subjected, took place many centuries later, viz.,
B.C. 680. Many had been the dynastic changes which
had taken place in the interim. Palestine had been
subjugated by the Thothmes, and lost under the
Sabacophs. The might of Rameses II. and III., the
fabled Sesostris of Grecian history, had spread itself
over Ethiopia, Arabia, and the islands of the Mediterranean, his conquering hosts had subdued even the
then rising city of Nineveh itself, and now from
Nineveh in turn, came the victorious son of Esarhaddon,
Assurbanipal, "king of countries, king of nations,"
to punish the Egyptian monarch Necho, who had
conspired with the maritime Phenicians to resist
the growing power of Assyria. By forced marches

[1] The ancient Crocodilopolis.

trampling under foot the rich harvest of the valley of the Nile, and reducing its denizens to a prospective famine, the monarch of Assyria reached the strongly fortified capital Thebes, in B.C. 664; after a short siege he took the capital, exercising upon its garrison the cruelties peculiar to his race; and the better to mark his conquest, removed two of the principal obelisks to his palace at Nineveh.[1] It is not stated from what temple these monuments were taken, and of course it is unknown now by whom they were erected; but this was the first instance in which an Egyptian obelisk suffered transportation. Bitterly did the land of the Pharaohs suffer for its monarchs' faithlessness, for the people of Thebes were banished to the city of Karbat, far from their favourite land, to dwell as serfs amidst a cruel nation; and the obelisks which had been worshipped, perhaps for centuries in the temple of Ra or Tum, were degraded to become the adornments of an Assyrian palace, and ultimately to be lost to the world for ever, by the destruction of Nineveh itself, B.C. 606.[2]

Much though the Greeks borrowed from the Egyptians in the domains of art and science, yet they do not seem to have been ever partial to the massive character of Egyptian architecture, and even if they adopted from the temples and tombs of Thebes the idea of the Doric and Ionic orders,[3] yet they never cared to introduce either for honour or ornament the monolithic obelisk; consequently neither Darius nor any of his Greco-Persian successors, attempted to

[1] *Records of the Past*, Vol. VI., gives the whole of the details of the Egyptian war.

[2] See Lenormant, *Anct. Hist.*, Vol. I., p. 416. There is now some doubt as to this first destruction of Nineveh by the *Medes*; till, however, the point is definitely fixed by the decypherment of inscriptions, the data must stand as they do.

[3] Notably the Doric order from the tombs at Beni-hassan; but there are some structural peculiarities which forbid the entire acceptance of the once popular theory.

3*

transplant any of the Egyptian obelisks to Europe.
This was the more remarkable, as the worship of the
sun god, under the names and attributes of Helios
and Phœbus, was an essential part of the Greek
mythology, as is proven alike by existing architectural
remains, and the *debris* of Hissarlik. Greco-Egyptian
pottery, and objects of household use, having a strongly
Egyptian character, were common enough in the best
furnished houses of Greece. Egyptian gods were
even introduced, but it was left for the Romans, to
whom nothing but power was sacred, and who knew
no power but Cæsar's, to follow the example of the
Assyrian tyrant, and to magnify the victories of
Augustus by spoiling the trophies of Pharaoh.

The first obelisk to be thus exiled to a western
city, was one which had been erected by Seti Menepthah I. before the temple of Ra; or, more probably,
Tum, at Heliopolis. This considered by Cæsar
as constituting an appropriate illustration of the conquest of Egypt, B.C. 30, and he therefore removed it
to adorn the centre of the Circus Maximus. Mindful,
however, of its sacred character, he upon re-erecting
it in Rome, renewed its dedication to the sun, as the
Latin inscription upon its base still testifies.

Augustus also removed, apparently a few years
later, a second obelisk, originally wrought by a king
whom Pliny calls Sesostris, perhaps also Seti I.; and
this he erected in the Campus Martius to serve as a
sundial, placing a gilded ball upon the summit in
order to render its shadow more distinct ; and for
a long season many curious astronomical data were
deduced from it. It, however, shared the common
fate of all the Roman gnomons, and was ultimately
thrown down and broken into four pieces, and was
in later years set up again in the Monte Citorio.'

The next emperor who followed the example of
Augustus, was Caius Claudius, who carried off two

' Pliny, Book xxxvi., Cap. 14.

lofty but uninscribed obelisks, A.D. 57; and with considerable trouble and expense had them again set up at the entrance of the mausoleum of Augustus: thus completely ignoring the fundamental intention of the original carvers of the monuments, and degrading the monoliths themselves into merely funereal ornaments.[1] The later Cæsars profited by the ruin of Egypt and the increase of mechanical skill, to transport to Italy more and more of the sacred stones of Egypt, adapting them almost solely to purposes of ornamentation; and there are now eleven obelisks still standing in Rome, most of which have been, however, set upright by the mediæval popes. There are, doubtless, several obelisks remaining still underground, but the chance of their disinterment is very problematical. One of them, long known to be lying under the ruins of Rome, was disinterred, A.D. 1740, by order of Benedict XIV.; and the original dedication of Augustus, "Soli donum dedit" discovered. The obelisk being found to be broken, and also to underlie the walls of one of the palaces, it was covered up again, and thus lost to the world. It was seventy-six feet in height.[2] Thus much then for the vicissitudes which have befallen the Egyptian obelisks, the next and remaining chapters must be devoted to an examination of each, according to the date of their construction.

CHAPTER V.

The Obelisks of Usirtescn at Heliopolis and Biggeg.

ON, or, as it was called by the Greeks, Heliopolis, the "City of the Sun," was one of the most

[1] See further on, Obelisks of Santa Maria Maggiore and Monte Cavallo.
[2] Murray's *Hand Book*, *Rome*, Ed. 1858.

ancient and most important of all the Egyptian
capitals ; it was famous for its temples, its palaces,
its fortifications, and its ecclesiastical schools, and so
great was its antiquity, that at the time of Joseph, when
it first became known to the Israelites by the residence
of the patriarch in the house of "Potipherah the
priest of On," it was already the second capital city
in the world.   It stood upon a lofty plateau of rocks
and sand, surrounded by deep canals and broad lakes,
bordered by papyrus meadows and sycomore groves.
On the north west stood the temple of the sun, which
had been founded by the monarchs of the first six
dynasties; in front of it were two lofty obelisks, and
an avenue of sphynxes; not far off, but sufficiently
distant to form a separate group, was placed the
temple of the bull god Mnevis, who shared together
with Ra the honour of being an eponymous god of
the Heliopolitan nome.   Despite all other attractions,
the chief glory of the city was its pair of red granite
obelisks, which, perfect alike in execution and propor-
tion, were erected before the pylon of the temple of
Ra by Usirtesen I., the first sovereign of the XIIth
dynasty.[1]   One of these two obelisks still remains to
attest to the power and piety of its founder, and the
skill of the architect and mechanics by whom it was
upreared.   The temples and shrine of Mnevis and of
Ra have been plundered, burnt, rebuilt, plundered,
destroyed, and rebuilt again and again by Hykshos,
Persian, and Roman, since the monolith was first
quarried from the rocks of Syene.   The contentious
Arab, and the idolent Turk, have pastured their
flocks in the sandy waste of what were once the
papyrus lakes of On ; bigotry, which hates with an
ignorant savageness all that it does not originate, and
war which levels in indiscriminating fury the works of
friend and foe alike, seem all to have spared at least
one of Usirtesen's gifts to the sun.   So singular is the

[1] Mariette's date for the foundation of the XIIth dynasty, is 2851 B.C.

circumstance of this one monument having survived the dynastic changes of the empire, that some antiquaries are inclined to believe that it is of later erection, if not a pious forgery of the XVIIIth or XIXth dynasty, since such a similar, and quite recent forgery exists at Rome, in the obelisk of Domitian in the Piazza Navona. There is no clear evidence that there is any real foundation for the conjecture. The obelisk may doubtless have been thrown down, as was also that of the Fayoum, and have been set up again in more peaceful times; but it is questionless the work of the monarch whose name it bears, and in all likelihood stands now where it was originally established four or possibly even five thousand years ago.

The following are the present dimensions of this obelisk : height 68 ft. 2 in.; eastern and west face, at the base, 6 ft. 3 in.; north and south faces, 6 ft. 1 in.; thus proving the fact, that even in the oldest examples there is no exact symmetery in the Egyptian monuments. It stands upon two broad steps, each about two feet high,[1] and down the centre of each face runs a line of beautifully carved and distinct hieroglyphics. The apex of the obelisk is somewhat damaged, as it has evidently been covered by a capping of gilded bronze; this covering remained intact when the ruins of Heliopolis were visited by the Arabian physician Abd-el-lateef, in the thirteenth century,[2] since he describes them in the following terms of admiration: "In this town are the two famous obelisks called Pharaoh's Needles ; they have a square base, each side of which is ten cubits long, and about as much in height, fixed on a solid foundation in the earth. On this base stands a quadrangular column of pyramidal form, 100 cubits high, which has a side of about 5 cubits

---

[1] Bonomi's proportions are 67 ft. 4 in., by nearly the same width as Wilkinson.

[2] Abd-el-lateef. De Sacy's translation, p. 180.

at the base, and terminates in a point. The top is covered with a kind of copper cap of a funnel shape which descends to the distance of three cubits from the top : this copper through the rain and length of time has grown rusty and assumed a green colour, part of which has run down along the shaft of the obelisk. I saw one of these obelisks that had fallen and broken in two owing to the enormity of the weight. The copper which had covered its head was taken away. Around these obelisks were many others too numerous to count, which are not more than a third, or a half as high as the large ones."

According to other Arabian historians cited by Long,[1] there was originally on the apex a figure of a man seated and looking towards the east. This was a common enough representation of itself ; and doubtless figured Usirtesen himself dedicating his obelisk to Ra ; the singular feature in the thing is that the apex bas-relief should have been of bronze, of which there is no existing example. The hieroglyphic inscription, which is a short one, and is nearly the same on each of the four sides runs thus :

" The Horus, the living from his birth,
    The king of upper and lower Egypt.
    Ra-Kheper-ka, lord of the two diadems, sun of the
        sun.
    Usirtesen, the loved of the gods of Heliopolis,
        living for ever ;
    The golden Horus, from his birth.
    The good god Ra-Kheper-ka,
    To the first celebration of the panegyry.
    He (has) made (this obelisk), the eternal generator."

The title of Horus was a usual one, and was borne by the kings of Egypt by virtue of their supposed royal birth as the result of a divine incarnation. " Lord of the two diadems, or of the *Shaa* and *Teshr*,"

---

[1] Long, *Egyptian Antiquities*, Vol. I., p. 48.

the crowns of the upper and lower countries respectively, meant, king of upper and lower Egypt. "Ra-Kheper-ka," or, "the Sun, the Creating Bull," was the divine name or prenomen of Usirtesen, as Usirtesen was his official and personal one; "The Eternal Generator" contains an allusion to the vivific power of Ra, as the creator of life. The festival or panegyry to which the inscription refers, is unidentified as yet. There were many such in the Egyptian Calendar;[1] it may possibly have been, so M. Brugsch thinks, the festival of leap-year, which there is some reason to believe was very anciently known to the Egyptians.

OBELISK OF BIGGEG (CROCODILOPOLIS).

Though the obelisk of Heliopolis is the only one that is now erect, yet there exists at Biggeg, or Crocodilopolis in the Fayoum, an obeliscoid monolith originally erected by Usirtesen; it cannot be properly called an obelisk, for it differs essentially in many details from the character of such an object, having a rounded summit with a deep groove in the middle, and its two sides or faces are disproportionately unequal, so that in section it resembles an oblong parallelogram; it is nearly 43 feet high, by 6 ft. $9\frac{1}{2}$ in. broad, and four feet thick; and now lies broken into two pieces; it is still regarded by the peasantry with superstitious reverence, and the barren fellaheen women recite their prayers at its side to remove the curse of sterility, as possibly did the men of Egypt for a similar purpose in a virile sense at its first erection.[2] As it now lies, only one face is visible, and

---

[1] Concerning this festival M. Chabas writes, "On n'est pas bien fixé sur, la nature de la fête. ⊙ 𓊪 𓏭 ⬭ 𓊃 𓊃 d'après la système de M. Brugsch, le serait la fête de la première année du quadriennième ramenant les années bissextiles."

[2] Murray's *Egypt*. M. Chabas gives the dimensions thus, height 25 metres, width 1. 71, depth 1. 02.

of this and of a translation of the hieroglyphics which are upon it, the following description is given by the distinguished Egyptologist M. Chabas, to whose courtesy most of these translations are due.

"The visible portion of the broad side consists of five scenes, or rather ten, in which the Pharaoh appears before ten pairs of divinities, five on the right, five on the left. This part of the inscription bears no legend but the name of the king and of the divinities, most of which are now illegible.

"Following these scenes, an inscription in nineteen columns commences with the titles of the king; but it is in so miserable a condition that no decypherment is practicable.

"The official legend was engraved on the narrow sides, the characters of which are clearly legible; they read:

North side.

"The heaven,
The kingly Horus,
Life of births,
Lord of the diadems,
Life of births.
King of Upper and Lower Egypt,
Ra-Kheper-ka, beloved of Pthah of *Res-sobt-ef* (Pthah of the southern wall),
The life of births,   .
Golden hawk,
Good god,
Master of Domination.

.   .   .   .

South side.

"The heaven,
The kingly Horus,
Life of births,
Lord of diadems,
Life of births,
King of Upper and Lower Egypt,

Ra-Kheper-ka,
Beloved of Month, lord of Thebais,
Life of births,
Hawk of gold,
Good god,
Lord of the two lands,
Lord of . . . . .

.   .   .   .   .   .

Besides these obelisks, Usirtesen erected several temples, both in upper and lower Egypt, and he was also the true founder of the great temple of Karnak at Thebes. He conquered the land of Cush or Ethiopia, and erected fortresses to repel the incursions of the negroes into Egypt. A great inundation of the Nile, followed by a famine, took place in his reign ; but the terrors of the drought were alleviated by the wisdom of one of his chief officers, named Ameni, whose funereal stele still remains to record his goodness. After reigning for thirty-eight years, Usirtesen associated his son Amenemha II. with himself in the government of the kingdom, thus reigning for four years longer ; and when he died, he left behind him a reputation which classed him for his bravery and piety among the demigod Pharaohs of Egypt.

CHAPTER VI.

The Obelisks of Thothmes I.

NEXT in antiquity to the obelisks of Usirtesen, but with an interval of many centuries between, come the monuments of Thothmes I., of the XVIIIth dynasty ;[1] and the principal of these monuments are the two huge obelisks which were erected

[1] Usirtesen was the son of Amenemha I., who was also called the first monarch of the XIIth dynasty; his name is variously written Usertesen, Seserten, and even Osirigesen by Sharpe.

before the temple of Amen Ra at Karnak. Of these, one has fallen, and lies prostrate on the sand; but the companion monolith is still standing, and is one of the most perfect in its proportions. Wrought out of the customary red granite of upper Egypt, it is 90 ft. 6 in. high, and bears upon each face a single column of hieroglyphics, containing its dedication to Amen Ra, by Thothmes, " Ra-aa-Kheper-ka (the sun, the great living bull), the son of the sun." The pyramidion at the apex, which is rather more acute than in the later examples, is also adorned with a votive vignette, and is the oldest illustration of that practice ; evidently, therefore, this obelisk was never designed for a metal covering,[1] but it may have had its summit gilded for the better preservation of the sculpture upon it.

Thothmes I. was one of the first of the Pharaohs of the revived empire, who endeavoured to enlarge the dominions of Egypt ; and the earliest inscriptions dated in his reign, record his conquest of Nubia, and his inroads upon the land of Khent-han-nefer, bringing back from thence ivory, gold, slaves, and cattle, which appear to have been the chief incentives to his expedition.[2] But the most illustrious of all his victories, were those which he obtained in the north, when, having subjugated the miscellaneous Canaanitish tribes of Palestine, he forced on his conquering armies to the frontiers of Nineveh, then the chief city of a confederation of Syrian nations, called the Rutennu ;[3] these subdued, he wasted the whole land of

[1] It may have been gilt, however, for its highly polished surface would not prevent such an application of the precious metal. In the Hay collection of Egyptian antiquities, now at Boston, U.S.A., there was a large fragment of well polished red Syenitic granite, having upon its surface the remains of gilding.

[2] Birch, *Egypt*, p. 82.

[3] The reign of Thothmes was the first which brought the Syrians, as distinct from the people of Palestine, into connection with Egypt.

Mesopotamia, to effect this crossing the desert with all his troops, and passing over the Euphrates at Karakamasha, or Carchemish,[1] one of the most important of the Syrian cities. On the banks of the Euphrates, as on the rocks at Tombos, the Egyptian monarch set up tablets recording his victories; and on his return from his Syrian wars introduced into his country the use of the horse and the war chariot, which afterwards became famous in history; for up to that time the only beast of burden in Egypt was the ass, and chariots were unknown : a palanquin being used to carry the sovereign upon occasions of state; while waggons drawn by oxen were the service of the peasant.[2] Thothmes reigned, according to some writers, twenty-one, and according to others, thirteen years; he left as his successor one daughter, Hatasu, and an infant son, Thothmes II., under her pupilage as regent. Thothmes was the Tuthmosis of the lists of Manetho; and his name denoted, "Son of Thoth," after the Egyptian god of letters and of arts: no unfitting deity to direct the energies of so great a king.[3]

CHAPTER VII.

The Obelisks of Hatasu.

IT is a magnificent compliment to the equality of her sex, and a compliment as true as it is magnificent, that whenever the sole government of a nation

[1] The Circesium of classical geography, and the site, according to the recent discoveries of the late George Smith, of an art and manufacture from which the designs of the Etruscans were derived.

[2] This fixes the period of Thothmes I. as being the earliest to which the Exodus of the Israelites can be assigned, as the horses and chariots of Pharaoh are particularly mentioned as taking part in it.

[3] I regret that I have not been able to obtain a translation of the inscription upon this obelisk in time for press.

falls into a female hand, it is generally administered
with remarkable ability, and is accompanied by undertakings of no less remarkable importance. Hatasu, or
Hat-scheps as her name is occasionally written, was
truly what that name denoted, "the first of noble ones."
She appears to have been the eldest child as well as
the daughter of Thothmes I., and in deference to the
feelings of the nation generally, during the first part
of the reign of Thothmes II. to have been nominally
associated with him as coadjutor rather than as
regent. The weakness of her brother soon induced her
to assume more and more the reins of power, and
after his death she became queen, both *de facto* and
de jure, taking the position of a man, and adopting on
state occasions the attire of one ;' and indisputably
no sovereign ever ruled over the dual kingdom with
more force and tact. The first event which signalized
her accession to the throne was the despatch of a large
fleet to the land of Ta-neter, or south-west Arabia, "The
Holy Land" according to the Egyptians, where were
obtained spices, perfumes, precious woods, and rare
flowers, and which was under the special protection
of Hathor, the Egyptian Venus. Till the time of
Hatasu, the Egyptians, to whom salt water was an
abomination and a defilement, as being the abode of
evil spirits, Egypt had no fleet to accomplish the
conquest of Arabia; Hatasu, however, caused some
ships to be built upon a Phenician model, and placed
the management of them under the guidance of
Phenician sailors, thus relieving the consciences of her
troops who had but to take their places and prepare
for the conquest of the Holy Land. Arabia subdued,

' The whole life of Hatasu, and her connections with her brothers
Thothmes II. and III., are involved in obscurity; according to some accounts she was both the sister and wife of Thothmes II., a custom which
frequently prevailed in Egypt, being sanctioned by the mythology which
made Isis the sister and wife of Osiris, whose characters both in theory
and in practice were assumed by the king and queen of Egypt.

and its queen brought captive to Hatasu, the Ethiopians, who had seized the opportunity of the reign of
a female sovereign to revolt, were defeated, and their
country permanently annexed; while the temple of
Deir-el-Bahri was erected in honour of Hathor and
as a record of Hatasu's successes.

The most beautiful of all the monuments of
Hatasu are the two great obelisks of red granite
which she erected in the second court of the temple
of Karnak, opposite to the great pylon of her father
Thothmes I. These are each of them over ninety-
seven feet high, and on all four sides as well as upon
their bases bear inscriptions setting forth the power
and devotion of the queen who dedicated them. Still
permanent and legible the beautiful symbolic script
of the Egyptian sculptor relates upon these obelisks,
that :[1]

"The queen, the pure gold of monarchs
 Had dedicated to her father, Amen of Thebes;
 Two obelisks of *mahet* stone (red granite),
 Taken from the quarries of the south,
 Their upper parts were ornamented with pure gold
 Taken from the chiefs of all nations.
 Her Majesty gave two gilded obelisks to her father
   Amen,
 That her name should remain permanent,
 Always and for ever in this temple.
 Each was made of a single stone of red *mahet*
   stone,
 Without joint or rivet.
 Her Majesty began the work
 In the fifteenth year of her reign,
 The first day of the month Mechir, of the sixteenth
   year,
 And finished it on the last day of the month Me-
   sore,

---

[1] Birch. *Egypt*, p. 85, 86.

Making seven months from its commencement in the quarry." [1]

On these obelisks also a kind mention is made of an infant sister, who is joined with Hatasu in the dedication; and it is further stated that the idea of causing these monoliths to be erected, "so that their tops should reach the heavens," came to the queen while seated in her royal palace, apparently by divine inspiration. These obelisks are further remarkable from their having a markedly designed *entasis*, which is unique in Egyptian art. The actual length of the reign of this mighty queen is not recorded upon the monuments, and there is considerable uncertainty respecting her latter end; it is certain that towards the close of her tenure of power her brother, a brother apparently by a later wife of Thothmes I., became associated with her as co-sovereign under the name of Thothmes III.; from that period they ruled together for at least sixteen years, which is the highest date at which the monumental stele mentions queen Hatasu; she then disappears from history for ever; and with a base ingratitude which implies a bitter resentment of years of control, Thothmes erased the name of his sister from every one of her edifices, and substituted his own cartouch for hers, alike on the walls of the palace, and the obelisks of the temple. It was beyond his power, petty as was his spite, and cruel as was his will, wholly to obliterate the evidences of his sister's glory, since the personal pronouns were allowed to remain in the original feminine gender; and from the nature of the hieroglyphics employed could not be altered into any other grammatical construction. The forgeries of Thothmes III. have, however, been thus far successful

[1] The month Mechir began about the 17th December, and Mesore about the 15th of June. The exact commencement of the month was uncertain, owing to the inconvenience of a travelling new year's day, and the interpolated Epagomenæ, the 24th to 28th of July.

that they have rendered the inscriptions on the Obelisk of Hatasu very difficult of decypherment; and it is almost impossible at this length of time to separate clearly the works of brother and sister, or to ascribe to each sovereign his or her respective part in the drama of archaic history.[1]

CHAPTER VIII.

The Obelisks of Thothmes III.

THE long reign of Thothmes III. marked the climax of Egyptian greatness, alike in her extent of empire and her commercial power. The armies of the south spread eastward, westward, and northward, in successive predatory expeditions. Thothmes I. had given to Egypt a regular army, Hatasu a navy, and to these Thothmes III. added a semi-royal mercantile system, sending his state-commissioned traders along specially levelled roads to purchase in all the markets of the world, while his ·troops preceded them to conquer, or followed them to annex. "Egypt," so ran the phrase on the monuments of the time, "set her frontiers where she pleased herself." The whole of the Syrian, Pales-tinian, and Arabian nations were overcome and forced to pay tribute. The crowning victory in the east, was the battle of Megiddo, in the plain of Esdraelon,[2] the perennial battle field of Palestine from that time to the present. Few people were

[1] Lenormant gives the height of 30 metres for these obelisks, and a weight of 374,000 kilogrammes, or 368 tons each.

[2] The battle of Megiddo took place on the 9th of the month Pachons, in the Neomenia of that month, in the twenty-third regnal year of Thothmes III. (Birch.) According to Lenormant the first of Pachons in the reign of this king fell about the middle of May.

killed, but a large number of prisoners were taken, besides a cavalry of 2132 horses, and 924 war chariots. The kings of Damascus, of Nineveh, and of Assur, all alike submitted costly presents; and abject tribute was sent to Egypt for the victor from every quarter of the then known world. In Africa his conquests spread beyond Ethiopia to Khartoum in the south,[1] and Algeria in the north ; the waters of the Black Sea were controlled by the sails of his fleet ; and the rivers of northern Europe rippled by the oars of his galleys. The walls of the pylons of Karnak enumerate more than one thousand different cities which paid him tribute; and the great god of Thebes, Amen-Ra, in an inflated address to the king, an address which is yet full of biblical images, is described as putting a sword into the hand of . the monarch wherewith he would

" Strike down Syrian princes,
  Under thy feet they lie throughout the breadth of
     their country,
  Like to the Lord of Light, I made them see thy
     glory,
  Blinding their eyes with light, the earthly image
     of Amen."[2]

It is not necessary here to even enumerate the victories, or to catalogue the long list of Egyptian buildings either founded or enlarged by Thothmes III. A monograph of his life would practically be a history of Egypt and the conterminous nations for half a century. The present interest of the great Pharaoh lies in his connection with the subject of the obelisks which he either altered or erected during

[1] In Maspero's *Histoire Ancienne des peuples de l'Orient*, is a capital map showing the extent of the empire of Thothmes III., an empire as great as any later sovereign ever ruled in suzerainty and not in confederation.

[2] *Lenormant*, Vol. I., p. 234. This version is a portion of that by M. de Rougé. A complete translation of the whole text is given by Dr. Birch in the *Records of the Past*, Vol. II., p. 23. *Second Edition.*

his eventful reign of fifty-four years. Not again to refer to those at Karnak which spuriously bear his name, the principal obelisks of Thothmes III., are those at Alexandria, at Rome, and at Constantinople, together with two small decorative obelisks bearing his cartouch at Karnak, but which may possibly in truth have been the work of his sister. These it were better to take in the order of magnitude than in that of position.

The great obelisk which now adorns the Piazza of St. John Lateran at Rome, was originally set up before the temple of Amen at Heliopolis; it is of red granite, and as it now stands it is 108 ft. 7 in. high, and its faces are respectively 9 ft. 8$\frac{1}{2}$ in. and 9 ft. wide at the base, one of the faces is slightly convex, and it has been calculated to weigh 455 tons.[1] The Persians, the Greeks, and the Romans, allowed it to remain in the place it was originally designed for, but on the establishment of Christianity, Constantine the Great intending it for the adornment of his new capital in the east, removed it to Alexandria[2] about 330 A.D.; this intention he was unable to carry out, but it was brought from Egypt by his successor, Constantius, who re-erected it in the Circus Maximus. A ship was built to convey the obelisk to Rome, three hundred rowers tugged the huge trireme with its ponderons burden across the waters of the Mediterranean to the shores of Ostia. Arrived there, the obelisk was slid off from the deck of the galley, on to a low cart supported by rollers instead of wheels, and it was then dragged and pushed through the gates of Ostia into the Circus Maximus.

"All that now remained to be done," records the historian, Ammianus Marcellinus, "was to set it upright, which they hardly expected to accomplish.

[1] Murray's *Hand Book*.
[2] Ammianus Marcellinus, Lib. xviii.

Large beams of wood were planted upright, and raised to a dangerous altitude, resembling a forest of machinery. To these were attached long thick ropes, which from their height and tension appeared but as so many slender threads, and veiled the sky as with a close netting. To these ropes the mountainous mass of granite, covered with its profusion of hiero-lyphics, was attached, and being gradually raised up into the air, and for some time actually suspended, was at last poised upon the base prepared for it, by the exertions of many thousands of men. A brazen sphere, covered with plates of gold, was placed upon the top, which, being soon after damaged by light-ning, and consequently taken away, was replaced by a figure of a flame, also made of brass, covered with gold leaf, and carved to resemble a blazing fire."[1] On the fall of Rome the obelisk was thrown down and broken into three pieces, and it was suffered to remain unnoticed, and indeed forgotten, save by a few antiquarians, amidst the ruins of the ancient circus till Pope Sixtus V. caused it to be excavated, re-stored and re-erected in the Piazza of St. John Lateran, A.D. 1588. Carlo Fontana, the famous architect, was employed to set it up again, and in order to enable it to stand it was found necessary to shorten the obelisk by four Roman palms, to obtain a level base.[2]

" Upon the pyramidion of the obelisk, on all four sides, is sculptured the same subject, differing only in the titles given to the god Amen, who presents to Thothmes III. the symbol of life ⳤ (the *crux ansata*), which with one hand he applies to the nostrils of the king, while with the other he holds the hand of the monarch." " A similar subject occupies the next compartment on all four sides, with this difference

[1] Ammian. Marcell., XVII., 4. Freely rendered.
[2] The Roman palm equals 8½ in. nearly.

only, that in these representations the god is seated, and the king is on his knees making an offering to the deity. On the two narrow sides of the obelisk the altar behind the throne of Amen is omitted." [1]

The upper portion of the obelisk is disfigured by several deep holes, apparently drilled by the Romans when they set it up in the Circus Maximus ; a defect in engineering skill which has disfigured the obelisk of the Porta del Popolo also, and reflects little credit upon the architects of a later day, who were unable without it to accomplish what the Egyptian mechanics had often successfully achieved a thousand years before. Another peculiarity in this monument is that the name of the god Amen, wherever it occurs is very deeply cut, and evidently was inserted in the place of some other figure, or the representation of some other deity which was purposely erased. This obliteration of the divine name we shall hereafter notice when describing the obelisks of Amenhotep II. and Rameses II.

The obelisk, although set up by Thothmes III., was probably not finished by him, as it was begun towards the close of his reign, and completed by Thothmes IV., who added the outer vertical lines of hieroglyphics, in which it is stated that the monolith was thirty-six years in the hands of the sculptor,[2] this affords a striking contrast to the rapidity with which the obelisks of Hatasu were excavated and set up. Subsequently this obelisk was thrown down in Egypt, since an inscription by Rameses II. records his re-erection of it.

The following is a translation of the entire hieroglyphic inscriptions, according to the authority of Dr. Birch.[3]

[1] Bonomi, *Trans. Soc. Lit.*, Vol. I., New Series, p. 161.

[2] Parker, *Obelisks of Rome*, p. 2.

[3] Published in *Records of the Past*, Vol. IV., p. 8.

Central line.

"The Harmachis,[1] the living sun,
The strong bull, beloved of the sun,
Lord of diadems, very terrible in all lands,
The golden hawk, the very powerful, the smiter of the Libyans,
The king Ra-men-kheper,
The son of Amen-Ra, of his loins,
Whom his mother Mut[2] gave birth to in Asher,
One flesh[3] with him who created him, the son of the sun,
Thothmes (III.) the uniter of creation, beloved of Amen-Ra,
Lord of the thrones of the upper and lower country,
Giver of life like the sun for ever."

South side, central line.

"The Har-em-akhu, the living sun,
The strong bull, crowned in Thebes,
Lord of diadems, augmenting his kingdom like the sun in heaven,
The hawk of gold, the arranger of diadems,
Very valiant, the king Ra-men-kheper,[4]
Approved of the sun, son of the sun,
Thothmes (III.) has made his memorial to his father Amen-Ra,
Lord of the seat of the upper and lower countries,
Has erected an obelisk to him
At the gateway of the temple before Thebes,
Setting up at first an obelisk in Thebes
To be made a giver of life."

[1] Harmachis was the divine name of the sun god Ra, as Ra in the horizon.

[2] Mut or Maut, was the great mother goddess of the Theban triad, Amen Ra-Mut, and Chonso.

[3] "Of the same substance as his father god."

[4] "Ra the giver of Life," prenomen of Thothmes III.

East side, central line.

"The Har-em-akhu, the living sun, beloved of the
    sun,
Having the tall crown of the upper region,
The Lord of diadems, celebrating the festival in
    truth,
Beloved on earth, the golden hawk,
Prevailing by strength, the king of the upper and
    lower country,
Ra-men-kheper, beloved of the sun,
Giving memorials to Amen in Thebes,
Augmenting his memorials,
Making them as they were before,
So that each should be as at first ;
Never was the like done in former times for Amen
In the house of his fathers,
He made, the son of the sun, Thothmes (III.),
Ruler of An, giver of life."

West side, central line.

"The Har-em-akhu, the living sun, the strong bull,
Crowned by truth, Ra-men-kheper,
Who adores the splendour of Amen in Thebes,
Amen welcomes him in . . . his heart
Dilates at the memorials of his son,
Increasing his kingdom as he wishes,
He gives stability and cycles to his Lord,
Making millions of festivals of thirty years,
The son of the sun, Thothmes (III.),
Uniting existence (giver of life)."

The two lines on each of the following sides refer
to Thothmes IV.

North side, right line.

" The good god, the image of diadems,
Establishing the kingdom like Tum,
Powerful in force, expeller of the nine-bow foreigners,
The king of the upper and lower country,

Ra-men-kheper,
Taking by his strength like the Lord of Thebes,
Very glorious like Mentu,[1]
Whom Amen has given strength against all countries;
The lands came in number,
The fear of him was in their bellies,
The son of the sun, Thothmes (IV.),
Diadem of diadems, beloved of Amen-Ra,
The bull of his mother."[2]

North side, left line.

" The king of the upper and lower country,
Beloved of the gods, adorer of the circle of the gods,
Welcomed by the sun in the barge,
And by Tum in the ark,
The Lord of the upper and lower countries,
Ra-men-kheperu,[3] who has ornamented Thebes for
ever,
Making memorials in Thebes.
The circle of gods of the house of Amen
Delight at what he has done,
The son of the god Tum, of his loins,
Produced on his throne, Thothmes (IV.), diadem of
diadems."

South side, right line.

" The son of the sun, Thothmes (IV.),
Diadem of diadems, set it up in Thebes,
He capped it with gold,
Its beauty illuminates Thebes ;
Sculptured in the name of his father, the good god
Ra-men-kheper (Thothmes III.),
The king of the upper and lower country,

---

[1] Mentu, a form of the sun god, as the Egyptian Mars.

[2] "The husband of his mother."

[3] Ra-men-kheper, singular, was the prenomen of Thothmes III., more generally written Men-kheper-Ra ; Ra-men-kheperu the same in the plural number, was the prenomen of his successor Thothmes IV.

Lord of the two countries,
Ra-men-kheperu (Thothmes IV.), did it
Wishing that the name of his father should remain
fixed
In the house of Amen.
The son of the sun, Thothmes (IV.) giver of life did
it."

South side, left line.

" The king of the upper and lower country,
The Lord doing things, Ra-men-kheperu,
Made by the sun, beloved of Amen.
His Majesty ordered that a very great obelisk should
be completed
Which had been brought by his father Ra-men-
kheper (Thothmes III.)
After His Majesty died.
This obelisk remained 35 years and upwards
In its place in the hands of the workmen
At the Southern quarters of Thebes.
My father ordered it should be set up.
I his son succeeded him."

East side, right line.

" Ra-men-kheperu (Thothmes IV.)
Multiplying memorials in Thebes of gold,
Lapis lazuli, and jewellery,
And the great barge on the river (named) Amen-
user-ta,
Hewn out of cedarwood which His Majesty cut
down in the land of Ruten
Inlaid with gold throughout,
And all the decorations renewed,
To receive the beauty of his father Amen-Ra
(When) he is conducted along the river.
The son of the sun Thothmes (IV.) diadem of
diadems, did it."

East side, left line.

" The good god, the powerful blade,
The prince taking captive by his power,
Who strikes terror into the Mena,[1]
Whose roarings are in the Anu.[2]
His father Amen brought him up,
Making his rule extended,
The chiefs of all countries
Are attentive to the spirits of His Majesty,
To the words of his mouth, the acts of his hands,
All that has been ordered has been done.
The king of the upper and lower country
Ra-men-kheperu, whose name is established in
Thebes, giver of life."

West side, right line.

" The king of the upper and lower country,
The Lord of the upper and lower world,
Ra-men-kheperu son . . . it making peaceful years,
Lord of the gods, who knew how to frame his plans
And bring them to a good end, who subdued the
nine-bow foreigners under his sandals,
The king of the upper and lower country . . .
Watched to beautify the monuments,
The king himself gave directions for the work
Like ' Him who is Southern Rampart,'[3]
He set it up, it remained for a while, his heart wished
to create it,
The son of the sun Thothmes (IV.), diadem of
diadems."

West side, left line.

" The king of the upper and lower countries
Ra-men-kheperu (Thothmes IV.) approved of Amen,
Dwelling amongst the chiefs,
Born in . . . him than every king,

[1] Asiatic shepherds.   [2] The Lybians.
[3] This is a title of the god Pthah of Memphis.

Rejoicing at seeing the beauty of his greatness;
His heart desired to place it.
He gave him the north and south submissive to his
    spirits,
He made his monuments to his father Amen-Ra,
He set up a great obelisk to him
At the upper gate, of Thebes, facing western Thebes.
The son of the sun whom he loves
(Thothmes IV.) diadem of diadems, giver of life he
    did it."

North side, inscription on pyramidion.

" The good god Ra-men-kheper like the sun.   Amen,
    Tum
The king of the upper and lower country,
Ra-men-kheper, son of the sun,
Thothmes like the sun, immortal.
Amen-Ra Lord of the seats of the upper and lower
    countries,
Gives all life stability, power."

South side, inscription on pyramidion.

" The king Ra-men-kheperu (Thothmes IV.)
Giver of life, beloved of Amen-Ra
Lord of the thrones of the two countries.
The son of the sun Thothmes (III.)
Giver of life like the sun for ever.
The king Ra-men-kheperu, son of the sun
Thothmes (III.) giver of life like the sun for ever.
The goddess Uat[1] gives a good life,
Amen-Ra Lord of the seats of the upper and lower
    country,
Gives life power and stability.
The good god Ra-men-kheperu
Giver of life like the sun.
Amen-Ra king of the gods (says)
' Thou hast received life in thy nostril.' "

[1] Uat or Buto was the goddess of the upper country.

East side, pyramidion.

" The good god Ra-men-kheperu,
  Giver of life like the sun
  The king Ra-men-kheperu, son of the sun
  Thothmes giver of life like the sun, gives water
  Amen-Ra king of the gods
  Gives life stability and power
  The good god Ra-men-kheperu,
  Giver of life,
  Gives a pyramidal cake of white bread
  That he may become a giver of life."

West side, pyramidion.

" Amen, Tum the good god,
  Ra-men-kheper giver of life like the sun immortal.
  The king Ra-men-kheper, son of the sun,
  Thothmes (III.), like the sun immortal gives wine.
  Amen-Ra Lord of the seats of the upper and lower
      countries,
  King of the gods, ruler of An.
  The good god, the Lord doing things, Ra-men-
      kheperu,
  Giver of life like the sun, gives incense
  That he may be made a giver of life."

At the base.

" Amen-Ra, Hor ; Lord of heaven Ra-user-ma,
  Approved of the sun, Rameses (II.) beloved of Amen
  Giver of life like the sun Amen-Ra, Lord of the seats
      of the upper and lower countries,
  Har-em-akhu, great god, Lord of the heaven
  The king of upper and lower Egypt,
  Lord of the two countries, Ra-user-ma,
  Approved of the sun Rameses (II.) beloved of
      Amen." '

' This records the restoration by Rameses II., and is a rare example
of an Egyptian sovereign, not arrogating to himself the honours of his
predecessor.

To these inscriptions may be added the following, consecrating the monument afresh to the honour of the Christian religion upon its re-erection by Sixtus V.:

SIXTVS V. PONT. MAX
OBELISCVM HVNC
SPECIE EXIMIA
TEMPORVM CALAMITATE
FRACTVM CIRCI MAX.
RVINIS HVMO LIMOQ.
ALTE DEMERSVM MVLTA
IMPENSA EXTRAXIT:
HVNC IN LOCVM MAGNO
LABORE TRANSTVLIT:
FORMAE. Q. PRISTINAE
ACCVRATE RESTITVTVM
CRVCI INVICTISSIMÆ
DICAVIT.
A.M.D. LXXXVIII. PONT. IIII.
FL. CONSTANTINVS
MAXIMVS AVG.
CHRISTIANAE FIDEI
VINDEX ET ASSERTOR
OBELISCVM
AB AEGYPTIO REGE
IMPVRO VOTO
SOLI DEDICATVM
SEDIB. AVVLSVM SVIS
PER NILVM TRANSFERRI
ALEXANDRIAM IVSSIT
VT NOVAM ROMAM
AB SE TVNC CONDITAM
EO DECORARET
MONVMENTO.[1]

---

[1] Parker, *Obelisks of Rome*, p. 6.

CHAPTER IX.

The Obelisk of Alexandria.

NEXT in size to the obelisk of the Lateran follow the two at Alexandria, which are popularly called, but erroneously, Cleopatra's Needles. These monuments were erected before the temple of Amen at Heliopolis by Thothmes III., and according to Pliny, whose statements must be taken with considerable reservation, Thothmes, or as he writes the name, Mesphres,[1] was "warned" to do so in a dream; "indeed there is an inscription upon the obelisk to this effect, for the sculptures and figures which we still see engraved thereon are no other than Egyptian letters."[2] Certainly the monarch may have been led by a dream to design the erection of these obelisks, but there is no record of the circumstance in the hieroglyphic inscriptions upon them. The obelisks are, one 70 ft. high by 7 ft. 7 in. wide, and the other 66 ft. the width being the same as its companion, both are of red granite, both stood on a limestone pedestal, 6 ft. 6 in. by 7 ft., resting upon three steps, and when first set up had only a single vertical column of inscriptions;[3] some years later the vain-glorious Rameses II. added two outside lines upon each face, while Seti II. also placed a few lines of hieroglyphics, together with his cartouch, on the lower part of the stone; and thus, as frequently occurs on the Egyptian monuments, the glories of more persons than the founders attach to them.

---

[1] According to Wilkinson, Mes-Phra Thothmosis was the manner in which, in the lists of Manetho, the name of the Pharaoh was written; but the words mean simply "sun born," or "son of the sun," and were a common title of all the Egyptian kings.

[2] Pliny, *Hist. Nat.*, Book xxxvi., Chap. 14.

[3] Pliny gives a height of 42 cubits, or 63 ft., Bonomi, 69 ft. 1 in.

The next notice of these obelisks comes on very late in history and brings us to the fall of a mighty empire, for in the eighth year of Augustus Cæsar, that sovereign being anxious to perpetuate the sense of his victory over the last of the Ptolemies, removed both monoliths from Heliopolis to Alexandria, and re-erected them in front of the temple called the Cæsareum, which he had himself founded, and which was for centuries one of the glories of Alexandria. This removal as we now know, took place during the prefecture of Pontus Rubrius Barbarus, who was the fourth prefect of Egypt under Augustus Cæsar. On attempting to re-erect the obelisks it was found that the lower portions had been so much corroded, and suffered so much dilapidation, this one especially, that the Roman engineers instead of imposing it flush upon its base, preferred to support the monolith upon four bronze crabs, or feet, each being about 16 in. in diameter, thus leaving a clear space of about 8 in. between the bottom of the obelisk and its pedestal. This plan, which was afterwards generally followed in Rome, caused the ultimate overthrow of all the obelisks set up by the Cæsars; first, on account of the inequality of the tension; and secondly, because the bronze was a metal too valuable to be suffered to remain when the period of ruin set in. In July of this year, Mr. John Dixon in clearing the soil from the fallen obelisk preparatory to its removal to London, excavated out also the base of the obelisk of Alexandria, and to the great satisfaction of antiquaries generally, discovered one of the bronze crabs which supported it still *in situ*, the others having long since been wrenched away. Upon this crab, or claw, were found on either side two inscriptions, one in Greek, the other in Latin, fixing precisely the date of the erection of the monument. The inscriptions are as follows :

Ε Η ΚΑΙΣΑΡΟΣ
ΒΑΡΒΑΡΟΣ ΑΝΕΘΗΚΕ
ΑΡΧΙΤΕΚΤΟΝΟΥΝΤΟΣ
ΠΟΝΤΙΟΥ

ANNO VIII.
AVGVSTI CAESARIS
BARBARVS PRAEF
AEGVPTI POSVIT
ARCHITECTANTE PONTIO.

"In the eighth year
Of Augustus Cæsar,
Barbarus, prefect
Of Egypt, caused this obelisk to be placed here,
Pontius being architect." [1]

Thus the votive monument of the Pharaohs sunk into
the condition of a Roman trophy, and that obelisk
which had been constructed at vast expense and labour
to record the majesty of the Egyptian empire, three of
whose greatest monarchs were associated with it, was
now by remorseless fate transported and transformed
to declare to the *Urbis Romanorum* the subjection of
the province of Egypt. It is obvious that as the
famous Queen Cleopatra died in the second year of
Augustus, while these obelisks were removed to
Alexandria in his eighth, or B.C. 23, that she could
have had nothing to do with the so-called Cleopatra's
Needle, and that consequently the connection of her
name with it is an anachronism and an absurdity.
Despite these facts, yet it is almost certain that that
popular tradition which has assigned to her the credit
of erecting the monument which was to testify to
her death and the destruction of her kingdom will remain ; and, historical facts notwithstanding, she will
doubtless continue to be credited with the erection of

[1] See Dixon's letter in *Daily News*, July 18, 1877; and illustration in
Graphic, July 7, 1877. The Latin text unfortunately differs in both; so
much for literal accuracy.

the first of the Egyptian monuments which meets the eye of a traveller, either from sea or land, on approaching the modern capital of Egypt. Only one of the two obelisks is now standing upon its pedestal, its companion having long fallen down, and after many centuries of neglect become the property of the British nation by the defeat of Napoleon in 1801. This, which will hereafter be better known as the Obelisk of London, deserves and will receive a chapter to itself further on.

OBELISK OF ALEXANDRIA.[1]

This obelisk was erected by the famous Thothmes III., whose legend is engraved in the central column of each side. During a period of no less than three centuries the monument existed with this legend only, till Ramses II. appropriated it to himself through the addition of two lateral columns, which were carved when the monolith was upon its base in the place first chosen by Thothmes III.

This Pharaoh dedicated it to Hor-em-akhou (Harmachis, or the sun at the two horizons), a form of the god Ra, or Phra (the sun), to which was also consecrated the great sphinx at Gizeh. The pyramidion represents a square vignette in which is figured the king seated upon a throne before the sphinx of Hor-em-akhou upon a pedestal.[2]

Central Columns. (Thothmes III.)

A. "The kingly Horus, lifting up the
Hat (*white crown*) ;
The king of upper and lower Egypt,

[1] Translated by François Chabas from the text in Burton's *Excerpta Hieroglyphica*, pl. 52.

[2] The copy of M. Burton is not perfectly reliable : therefore the translation will possibly require a few amendments in some passages. Moreover two of the sides are in a very bad state of preservation, and the script there is undecypherable. Here I give all that I can read on the erect obelisk.

Golden hawk, ...
Who has struck the kings of
All lands approaching him ;
After the commandment
Of his father Ra.[1]
Victory over the entire world,
And valiance of sword are at the mouth
Of his hands,[2]
For the extension of the limits
Of Egypt,
The son of the sun,
Thothmes, vivifier."

B. " The kingly Horus,
Strong bull, crowned in Thebes,
The Lord of diadems,
Whose royalty is expanded,
Like (that of) the sun.
(Beloved of Tum,[3] Lord of Heliopolis,
Son of his loins,
Thoth created him, Thothmes.) [4]
They [5] created him in the great abode,
From the perfection of their limbs,
So that he will make an extended royalty for
　　centuries.
The king of upper and lower Egypt,
Ra-men-Kheper
Beloved of Tum, the great god,
And the gods of his circle,
Giving all life, stability, and happiness,
Like the sun for ever."

C. " The kingly Horus,
Strong bull, crowned in Thebes,

[1] The sun.
[2] " The mouth of the hand," is an expression similar to " the mouth of the
blade."
[3] Tum or Atum is a name of Har-em-akhou.
[4] This cartouche is very curious and interesting, as the phrase is calculated to form the name of Thothmes with the last word of each column.
[5] Thoth and Tum.

The king of upper and lower Egypt,
Ra-men-Kheper,
(*The remainder is illegible.*)
D. The same as C. Nothing further can be read.

Lateral Columns. (Rameses II.)

A 1 "The kingly Horus,
Strong bull, son of Tum,
The king of upper and lower Egypt,
The Lord of diadems
Who protects Egypt and chastises the nations,
Son of the sun,
Ramessou, Meriamen,
King, warlike,
Who has acted with his own hands
In the face of the whole earth,
The Lord of the two lands,
Ra-ousor-ma-Sotep-en-Ra,[1]
Son of the sun,
Ramessou Meriamen,
The stable" (*the rest erased*).
A 2 "The kingly Horus,
Strong bull, beloved of the goddess Ma,
The king of upper and lower Egypt,
Ra-ousor-ma-Sotep-en-Ra,
Lord of panegyries like his father[2]
Ptah Totanen,
Son of the sun,
Ramessou Meriamen.
Ra[3] has generated him
To adorn festively Heliopolis,
To furnish abundantly the temples
Of him who generated him.
The Lord of the two lands,
Ra-ousor-ma-Sotep-en-Ra,
Son of the sun,

[1] Prenomen of Rameses II.
[2] "Lord of Festivals," *i.e.*, the annual sacred feasts.   [3] The sun.

5*

Ramessou Meriamen
(invested with life) stability and happiness."
B 1 "The kingly Horus,
Strong bull, beloved of Ma,
The king of upper and lower Egypt,
Ra-ousor-ma-Sotep-en-Ra
(Who is) a sun, generator of gods,
Possessor of the two lands,
Son of the son,
Ramessou Meriamen,
A noble youth of kindness
Like Aten [1]
Blazing from the horizon.
Lord of the two lands,
Ra-ousor-ma-Sotep-en-Ra,
Son of the son,
Ramessou Meriamen,
The splendour of Osiris,
Vivifier."
B 2 "The kingly Horus,
The strong bull, son of Kheper-Ra,[2]
The king of upper and lower Egypt,
Ra-ousor-ma-Sotep-en-Ra,
Golden hawk,
Of abundant years,
(Very) victorious,
Son of the sun,
Ramessou Meriamen,
Who issued from the womb
To take the crowns of the sun ;
Whom the sun generated to be (the)
Sole Lord, Lord of the two lands,
Ra-ousor-ma-Sotep-en-Ra,
Son of the sun,
Ramessou Meriamen,
The splendour of Osiris,
Like the sun."

[1] The solar disk.　　　　　[2] The creator.

It is to be observed that the final groups of the three columns are combined to form a horizontal line, running thus : "Giving life for ever, like the sun." This is observable in three sides, the fourth being erased.

C 1 "The kingly Horus,
Strong bull, beloved of Ma,
The king of upper and lower Egypt,
Ra-ousor-ma-Sotep-en-Ra,
(Who is) a sun, generator of gods,

. . . . . .

Lord of the two lands,
Ramessou Meriamen . . . ."
(*The remainder is illegible.*)

C 2 "The kingly Horus,
Strong bull, son of the sun,
The king of upper and lower Egypt,
Ra-ousor-ma-Sotep-en-Ra,
Golden hawk,

. . . . . .

Son of the sun,
Ramessou Meriamen,"
(*Erased.*)

D 1 (*Erased.*)

D 2 "The kingly Horus,
Strong bull, beloved . . . .
The king of upper and lower Egypt,
Ra-ousor-ma-Sotep-en-Ra,
Lord of panegyries
Like his father Ptah, Lord of . . . .
Ramessou Meriamen."

Some words are still distinguishable, but nothing worth mentioning can be read in the remainder of the text.

It is worth notice that a very carefully measured elevation of this obelisk is given in Denon's *Egypte*, representing it as standing upon a square pedestal supported upon three steps, adding 3 ft. 2 in. further to the height of the obelisk. This, as far as its goes, is all very well, but it is doubtful what reliance ought to be placed upon the plates in the great French work, since if Denon actually uncovered the base of the monolith he must have noticed the bronze crab which was discovered by Mr. Dixon ; and he must further have seen the dilapidated condition of the angles of the obelisk, whereas neither of these points is represented in his plates.

CHAPTER X.

The Obelisk of Constantinople.

ANOTHER large obelisk set up by **Thothmes III.** is that which recorded his victories in Meso-potamia, and which was also originally one of the splendours of Karnak ; it was subsequently carried off by Constantine the Great to decorate the hippo-drome[1] of Constantinople, and there it still remains. Apparently it has become broken during transit, for its present height is only 50 ft., and it is about five dia-meters high; the base is now concealed in the ground, but evidently if the monolith were perfect it would be one of the loftiest of its kind, and be a rival to that of Thothmes I. at Karnak. When it was set up by the Emperor Theodosius, circa A.D. 379, it was placed by the Prætor Proclus upon four brazen balls, and its angles were repaired by insertions of Theban porphyry. A base or pedestal of wrought stone, 12 ft. broad, and 4 ft. 8 in. high, was also added, and the sides were adorned with a series of bas-reliefs representing the mechanical contrivances employed in raising up the monument, where the emperor and

[1] The At-Meidan.

the architect are figured directing the numerous workmen, some of whom seem to be adorning the obelisk after its erection.[1] On the other face of the pedestal are two inscriptions, one in Greek and one in Latin, both of which are now illegible, but from which we learn that the whole operation of raising and fixing the obelisk took thirty-two days. The following are the inscriptions as copied by Hobhouse and Gyllus:

> Difficilis quondam dominis parere serenis
> Jussus et extinctis palmam portare tyrannis
> Omnia Theudosio cedunt sobolique perenni
> Ter denis sic victus ego domitusque diebus
> Judice sub Proclo superas elatus ad auras.

" I was once unwilling to obey imperial masters,
But I was ordered to bear the palm after[2] the destruction of tyrants.
All things yield to Theodosius and his enduring offspring.
Thus I was conquered and subdued in thirty days,
And elevated towards the sky in the Prætorship of Proclus." [3]

> Κίονα τετράπλευρον ἀεὶ χθονὶ κείμενον ἄχθος
> Μοῦνος ἀναστῆσαι[4] Θευδόσιος βασιλεὺς
> Τολμήσας Πρόκλῳ ἐπεκέκλετο, καὶ τόσος ἔστη
> Κίων ἠελίοις ἐν τριάκοντα δύο [5]

Like that obelisk, too, it has a sculptured apex and a single vertical column of hieroglyphics upon two only of its sides, the lower portion of which is lost; it is of red granite, and has not as yet been sufficiently uncovered

---

[1] Figured in Gyllus' *Antiquities of Constantinople*, Ed. Ball, 1729, pl. 8.

[2] To commemorate the victory over.

[3] Hobhouse, *Travels*, p. 951.

[4] It was doubtless this previous fall which reduced the obelisk to its present dimensions.

[5] Long, *Egypt. Antiq.*, I., p. 332.

to allow of the entire inscription being decyphered. Enough of the text remains to prove that the obelisk was really erected by the monarch whose name it bears, though the Emperor Theodosius has had the credit of having ordered it to be imitated from an earlier work ; the general consensus of Egyptologists is now opposed to such a theory, since the historical record upon it does not exist elsewhere so characteristically summarised.

Each of the four faces of the apex show a square scene, in which Thothmes III., standing up, takes the hand of Amen, who presents to the nose of the king the so-called cross of life, ♀. In two places the king wears the crown of upper Egypt, white crown ⌀ ; and in the two others that of lower Egypt, red crown ☡.

Similarly the god wears in two places the double feathered crown ⌀ ; and in the two others, the *pschent* ☡, or double royal crown of Egypt.

Amen appears in his two principal characters of Lord of the thrones of the two lands, and of Amen-Ra, king of the gods, Lord of earth.

At the head of each of the inscriptions on the vertical sides another square vignette represents the king on his knees, before Amen sitting upon a chair.

The king offers four sorts of presents, among which wine and milk are still distinguishable, and the god imparts to him life and happiness in the usual style.

The inscriptions of those square scenes are quite commonplace. It will suffice to translate that of the east side, which is in a good state of preservation.

The following translation of the upper portion of the columns is by M. Chabas :'

' The obelisk itself is published in Lepsius, *Denkmäler aus Ægypten*, Abth. III., Bl. 24.

Over the king sitting down.

" Amen, Lord of the thrones of the two lands,
    Dwelling (in Thebes), great god,
    He gives all life, all happiness, all stability."

Over the kneeling Pharaoh.

" The good god, Lord of the earth,
    Master of making things,
    The king of upper and lower Egypt,
    Ra-men-kheper, son of the sun,
    Thothmes, giving all life, like the sun, for ever."

The following is, as translation, the tenor of the four vertical lines in the order of M. Lepsius's plates.

West Side.

" The heaven, the kingly Horus,
    Strong bull, swaying through truth,
    The king of upper and lower Egypt,
    Ra-men-Kheper-iri-em-Ra,[1]
    Who has gone through the great circuit of Naharana,
    In strength and victory, at the head of his troops,
    Making a great slaughter . . . . . ."

South Side.

" The heaven,
    The kingly Horus,
    The strong bull, swaying through
    Truth,
    The Lord of diadems,
    Enlarging royalty,
    Like the sun on high
    The golden hawk,
    Of hallowed diadems,
    Warlike dominator,
    King of upper and lower Egypt,

---

[1] Firm existence of the sun; creature of the sun.   [2] Mesopotamia.

Ra-men-Kheper-Sotep-en-Ra,[1]
He made (the obelisk) in
His monuments to his father,
Amen-Ra, Lord of the thrones of
The two lands.
He erected . . . . .

East Side.

" The heaven,
The kingly Horus,
Uplifting the white crown,
Beloved by the sun,
King of upper and lower Egypt,
Lord of diadems,
. Swaying through truth,
The love of the two lands :
Ra-men-Kheper, son of the sun,
Lord of victory,
Chastiser of the whole earth,
Who has set his boundary
At the horn of the earth.
And at the extremities of Naharana . . . .

(Here the term, horn of the earth, refers to the
southern mountains, and the extremities of Naharana
to the northern limit of Egypt at the time.)

South Side.

" The heavens,
The kingly Horus,
Strong bull,
Beloved by the sun,
The king of upper and lower Egypt,
Ra-men-Kheper, whom Kheper-Ra has magnified,
Nursling of Tum,
Foster-child
In the arms of Neith, the

[1] Approved by the sun.

Divine mother ;
As a king ;
He has conquered all lands.
Protracted (is) his life ;
Lord of the feasts of 30 years . . . . ."[1]

This monument is highly illustrative of the glory
of this famous reign.   Egypt was then invested with
the domination of all civilized nations, from Armenia
and the Caucasus, down to Central Africa.[2]

Besides these colossi there are standing at Karnak
two small obelisks of red granite, each about 20 ft.
high, they differ from the ordinary obelisks inasmnch
as they bear a pictorial representation of the lotus of
Lower Egypt, instead of hieroglyphics.   Neither of
them have any pyramidion, or if they ever had one it
has disappeared ;   the cartouche of Thothmes III.
upon the vertical sides fixes the date of the monuments to the reign of that king, who seems to have
set them up more for decorative than religious purposes.   Thothmes III. after filling Egypt with his
monuments, Asia with his exiles, and Arabia with
his traders, was succeeded by Amenhotep II., a
monarch of a wholly different character, whose
relationship to Thothmes is not known, and whose
reign was either so short or so uncertain, that the
lists of Manetho do not notice him, and he is known
only by the historical inscriptions.[3]

There is also a small red granite obelisk of
Thothmes III. at Sion House, but it has not yet
been published.   It came from Elephantine.

[1] The triaconterides, one of the most famous of the cyclical festivals of
the Egyptians.

[2] In the inner Sanctuary of Karnak is a fine bas-relief, representing
Thothmes III. offering these obelisks with other treasures to Amen-Ra.
The figure was originally that of his sister Hat-a-su, whose head was
chiselled out to insert that of her more imperious brother.   Wilkinson,
Thebes, p. 179.

[3] Lenormant, I., p. 236.

CHAPTER XI.

The Obelisk of Amenhotep II.

SHORT as was the reign of Amenhotep II., and few as were his official acts, yet he appears to have made an effort to retain the conquests of his predecessor, and to have had some desire of encouraging the arts. The chief events in which he took part as sovereign were the suppression of a revolt in Mesopotamia, the re-imposition of tribute upon the people of Nineveh, and the chastisement of the Ethiopians. An inscription in the temple of Amada in Nubia, relates that he fought with his enemies in the land of Asshur; that seven kings fell before him, and were brought (their embalmed bodies, it is to be supposed) to the banks of the Nile, where six were hung against the wall of Thebes, and the seventh at Napata, the capital of Ethiopia, "that the negroes might see the victories of the ever-living king over all lands and all people upon earth, since he had possessed the people of the south, and chastised the people of the north." [1] The reign of Amenhotep II. is also marked by a peculiarly exaggerated style of drawing and modelling the human figure, the rigid, but beautiful proportions of the canon of Thothmes III., a copy of which is still in the British Museum, [2] were disregarded, and an attempt at anatomical naturalness in the form of the muscles, and of fulness in the chest and legs, characterises the style of this period, a style which is most marked and most defective in the portrait statues of the king, and the high officers of his court. [3]

[1] Lenormant, I., p. 236.

[2] For the details of the canon as compared with the Greek canon of Polycletus, the assumed normal standard of excellence, see Bonomi, *Proportions of the Human Figure.* (Original edition.)

[3] This was still more developed in the reign of Amenhotep III. For examples of these affectations of art, see the statues figured in Sharpe's *Antiquities in the British Museum*, p. 33-50.

Amenhotep II. does not seem to have erected any important obelisks, or if he did, they were thrown down and destroyed in the religious revolution caused by the sole worship of Aten-Ra, under his next successor but one, Amenhotep IV.[1] But there is in this country a small obelisk bearing the name of Amenhotep, and differing in several respects from the more usual examples. This obelisk was discovered in or about 1838, in the *debris* of a ruined village in the Thebaid, and it was presented to the late Duke of Northumberland, then Lord Prudhoe, by the Viceroy of Egypt. The original location of the relic is not ascertainable ; it is of red granite, and (its apex being broken) stands 7 ft. 3 in. high, its greatest width is 9¾ in. on two of the sides, and 9 in. on the others, it is inscribed only upon one face, and the hieroglyphics are not cut with an inner rounded contour, as was always done in the XVIIIth and XIXth dynasties, but their inner surfaces are left flat, " a kind of sculpture found only in tombs and on stelæ, generally of the age of Psammetichus ;"[2] indeed, were it not for the fact that the letters of the name of Amen in the cartouch of the king have been re-cut over the hieroglyphs of some other

[1] This revolution belongs purely to the theological history of Egypt, it was brought about by the marriage of Amenhotep III., the Memnon of the Greek historian with a Semitic lady named Taia, who introduced the worship of the sun's disk without any material representation, to the ultimate entire overthrow of the ancient faith in the reign of her son Amenhotep IV., or Chu-en-Aten as he preferred to be called, resigning his Pharaohnic title "peace of Amen," for "glory of Aten," *i.e.*, the solar disk. It is believed that the obliteration of the name of Amen on the monuments of Egypt took place during his reign. After a half century of ill-borne religious tyranny, the dynasty of Amenhotep was overthrown, the old worship of the gods restored, and their statues set up again; every vestige of the foreign faith was obliterated, and the name and statues of Chu-en-Aten and his mother destroyed, and their temples pulled down to re-build those of Amen-Ra and Tum once more.

[2] Bonomi on "The Alnwick Obelisk," *Trans. Roy. Soc. Lit.*, Vol. I., New Series, p. 174.

divjne name, the obelisk might be attributed to the period of the **XXVIth** dynasty, not to the **XVIIIth.** The hieroglyphics read as follows :[1]

Translation of the Obelisk at Alnwick.

This obelisk was erected by the Pharaoh, Amen-hotep II., whose royal Egyptian names were **Ra-aa-Kheperou** and **Amen-hotep-hik-An.** It reads :

Vertical Column.

" The heaven,
The Horus, king of the two lands, sun of life,
Strong bull,
Very valiant,
King of upper and lower Egypt,
Ra-aa-Kheperou,[2]
Son of the sun,
Amen-hotep-hik-An,[3]
He made (the obelisk)
In his monuments to his father Num-Ra ;
Making to him two obelisks . . . . with the food
   of Ra.[4]
He made it,
The vivifier, for ever."

At the Apex of the Obelisk.

" The heaven,
Homage to Num.
He gives all life and bliss,
(To) Amen-hotep, the vivifier, for ever."[5]

After this reign the kingdom of Egypt was in too disturbed a condition to admit of the execution of any

[1] The translation is by M. Chabas.
[2] Sun, the greatest of existences.
[3] The peace of Amen, sovereign of Heliopolis.
[4] The sun. The obelisks were objects of worship. Priests were attached to them; therefore the erection of these monoliths was connected with the endowment of a religious service, especially with the necessary supply of offerings. This accounts for the mention of the *table* or *food* of Ra. Note by M. Chabas.
[5] Published by Sharpe, *Egyptian Inscriptions*, Second Series, pl. 69.

great works.   Amen-hotep III., though one of the most able of Egyptian monarchs, confined his attention to hunting and schemes for the irrigation of the country, the chiefest of which was the construction of a vast reservoir 3400 cubits long by 700 broad.[1] He built a large number of temples, and is still remembered by the two colossi, representing himself and his queen, which overlooks the Lybian valley, and the largest of which was known afterwards to the Greeks as the Vocal Memnon. Fond as he was of grandeur, Amenhotep set up no obelisks ; possibly his queen, who was a Syrian heretic, according to Egyptian notions, dissuaded him from so doing, as she was desirous of introducing a totally opposite form of solar adoration. His son was a revolutionist, a reformer, and a heretic, and his reign was a brief and turbulent one. The daughters of Amenhotep IV., and their husbands, divided, or tried to divide, the empire between themselves ; then followed internecine war and family schisms, a second religious revolution, and ultimately the rise of a new dynasty connected by marriage with the last Pharaoh of the preceding. This dynasty, the XIXth, was destined to witness the culmination and incipient decline of Egyptian greatness ; and it is the obelisks of these sovereigns, the half-Semitic Pharaohs of the Rhamesside family, that next demand attention, and which are still the most noted in existence.

CHAPTER XII.

The Life of Seti I.

THE two first monarchs of the XIXth dynasty, Kames, and Rameses I., do not appear to have

[1] About 5000 by 1000 English feet.

erected any obelisks; but the son-in-law, and successor
of this last sovereign, an Egyptian general of
Semitic origin, signalised his reign by a return to the
erection of the ancient symbols of the worship of the
sun.   Seti, or Seti-Menepthah I., was, it has now
been clearly established, a descendant of one of those
Hykshos princes, whose posterity still remained as
agriculturists in the Delta.[1]   In fact the expulsion of
the Hykshos had never been so complete as to have
driven the entire body of the people beyond the
frontiers of Egypt; their kings were slain and their
power broken; but a large number of the foreigners who
had intermarried with the Egyptians, and had become
assimilated with them through the domestic fusion of
thirty generations, staid behind, incorporating the
worship of the land of the Nile with the Set cultus of
their Palestinian brethren.[2]

During the religious troubles which closed the period
of the XVIIIth dynasty, the Semites seem to have
maintained their position securely as an allied, rather
than a dependent race; and Seti I. was apparently the
son of one of their chiefs, who became a confederate of
Rameses I., in whose armies he himself acted as a
general.   On the death of his master, he was regarded
by the native legitimate Egyptians simply as a
regent acting on behalf of his son Rameses II., who
was called "king in the womb of his mother before
he was born;" but practically the genius and warlike achievements of Seti constituted him the sole
sovereign of the upper and lower kingdom for nearly

[1] Lenormant, I., p. 240.
[2] Set or Sutekh, a kind of ass-headed deity, was the local god of the
nations of the Hittites and Canaanites; the earlier Egyptians equated him
with their one good deity Set, who was afterwards identified with Typhon,
the brother and adversary of Osiris, and the evil being *par excellence*.
Still, despite of all changes, Set retained a position in both theologies,
though his name was carefully erased from the monuments of the
Ramesside kings.

half a century, the latter years of which were passed in that happy condition of national peace and prosperity which leaves no mark on the registers of history.[1]

As a conqueror, the chiefest victories of Seti I. were over the Rotennu, and their allies in northern Syria; over the Shasu, or Arabs, who had invaded Egypt on the frontier towards Suez; over the Lybians in the north west; and lastly, over the Ethiopians in the south. These were almost the hereditary foes of the Egyptians; for Ethiopia and Mesopotamia occupied in Egyptian politics a similar position to that taken by the Scots and French in the mediæval period of English history. All his enemies, however, Seti-Menepthah overcame. The Hittites he gave battle to in the valley of the Orontes, and finally defeated both them and the Amorites by the capture and battle of Kadesh, the capital of the Hittites. The Rotennu with their allies, the kings of Nineveh, Babylon, and Singar, were reduced again to the position of tributaries, as the result of a long campaign in the· mountains of Armenia; and in the end the whole of the Asiatic conquests of Thothmes III. were recovered, with the exception of the maritime provinces, which the now rising naval power of the Pelasgian nations enabled them to withhold from the grasp of the Pharaohs. As an internal administrator and politician, Seti took a high rank; the navy originally instituted by queen Hatasu, but which during the troublous seasons which followed her decease had been neglected and its materials scattered, was reconstructed; the gold mines in the Arabian deserts, hitherto unworkable from the sterility of the soil, were again opened up, and an artesian well sunk with great success to supply the miners with water, an undertaking which was recorded by the priests in language which to us appears

[1] There are no dated monuments of the reign of Seti-Menepthah later than his thirtieth year, but the lists of Manetho assign to him a reign of fifty years duration.

idolatrous, as ascribing the rush of water to the miraculous power of the simple words of command of the monarch in person.[1] Last, and greatest in its conception of all the undertakings of Seti, was the excavation of a canal from the Isthmus of Suez to the Red Sea, passing the city of Zat, the Heroopolis of the Greeks, on the line of what has been again known to an admiring world as the Suez Canal. The bas-reliefs, describing the victories of Seti, in the Hall of Columns at Karnak, have left to posterity, among other historical notices, this most striking proof of the wisdom and the power of the half usurper king of Egypt.

The architectural works of Seti were very numerous; the whole of the great temple at Karnak, including the gigantic Hall of Columns, a hall in which the loftiest conceptions of modern architecture are over-powered, and the great temple tomb of Osiris at Abydos, a temple which was more than 560 feet long, the palace of Kurnah, and many lesser palaces, were all begun, and nearly completed by him. Actuated by a similar spirit of magnificence, he caused during his lifetime, his own tomb to be prepared in the valley of the tombs of the kings, the modern Biban-el-Moluk at Thebes, like the temple of Karnak of which no written description can give an adequate idea. This tomb was, and indeed still is, one of the wonders of the world;[2] it contained a series of exquisitely sculptured and painted chambers, extending for more than 300 yards into the depth of the mountain. His sarcophagus was wrought out of a monolith of the purest arragonite; a translucent species of veined alabaster; and it was adorned with a selection of chapters from the mystical Book of Hades, one of the

---

[1] See Birch, "Inscription of the Gold Mines of Rhedesieh," *Records of the Past*, Vol. VIII., p. 67.

[2] It was first opened by Belzoni, in October 1815, who on his return to England, set up a model of one of the principal chambers in a hall in the Egyptian Museum, Piccadilly, now the Egyptian Hall.

most occult books in the whole range of Egyptian mythology. These inscribed texts which were afterwards filled in with blue oxide of copper, covered the coffin both within and without ; and in the chambers around the sarcophagus were deposited many hundred of Shabti, or funereal figures of the deceased monarch in the character of Osiris, which had been left there for the benefit of his soul by his devoted officers and friends.[1]

Unfortunately for the honour of this great Pharaoh, his son Rameses II. by placing his own name upon the monuments of Seti, deprived his father of the credit that should have been attached to him. Unhappily also, his great temple at Abydos has almost wholly fallen into ruins, his palace at Kurnah has shared the like fate, and his own tomb was invaded by the Persians under Cambyses, who broke open the royal sarcophagus, destroyed its covering, and threw away, or destroyed also, the royal mummy which it contained. None of his Egyptian obelisks remain in the land of their erection, and the largest of them is that which now stands in the Porto del Popolo at Rome, and is named the Flaminian Obelisk, after the name of the Roman imperial family in whose circus it was set up.

CHAPTER XIII.

The Obelisk of the Porta del Popolo; or, the Flaminian Obelisk.

THIS magnificent obelisk was one of two which originally were erected by Seti I. before the

[1] A full description of the Sarcophagus of Seti I., which is now the chief treasure of the Soane Museum in Lincoln's Inn Fields, is given in Bonomi, *Sarcophagus of Oimenepthah I.;* a translation of the text with which it is covered will appear in the next volume (Vol. X.) of the *Records of the Past*, and will be written by M. Lefèbure, who has devoted the energies of a scholar's lifetime to the elucidation of the more obscure Egyptian myths.

temple of Amen-Ra at Heliopolis, and the centre column of hieroglyphics was intended to perpetuate the remembrance of the Asiatic victories of the founder. Rameses II. with the usual ingratitude of Egyptian sovereigns towards their predecessors, added two outer columns of hieroglyphics, arrogating to himself the re-dedication of the monument; and it is probable that at the same time he caused the objectionable figure of the Syrian deity Set to be chiselled out of the first part of the cartouch of his father, and a seated figure of the god Ra sculptured in its place. Carefully as was this alteration carried out it could not be wholly effectual, and the result has been in some places that the long square ears, which characterised the head of the hated god, appear above the hawk's head of the Egyptian deity. On the conquest of Egypt, Augustus Cæsar had it removed to the Circus Maximus at Rome, in his twelfth year, B.C. 20, and re-dedicated it to the sun, on which occasion he caused the following inscription to be incised upon its base :

IMP CAESAR DIVI F
AVGVSTVS
PONTIFEX MAXIMVS
IMP XII. COS XI. TRIB POT XIV.
AEGYPTO IN POTESTATEM
POPVLI ROMANI REDACTA
SOLI DONVM DEDIT.

During the wars and conflicts which took place in the city of Rome after the decadence of the empire of the Cæsars, the obelisk was overthrown and broken into three pieces, in which condition it remained in the reign of Valentinian, circa A.D. 364. Buried and forgotten it rested beneath the soil, or was trodden under foot, through all the struggles of mediæval Rome, till the Pontificate of Sixtus V., who set it up afresh, A.D. 1590, and consecrated it to the service of

Christianity by adding a gilt ball and cross at its summit, and a long inscription upon its ancient base, beneath the space occupied by the inscription of Augustus, which in perspicuity and brevity far exceeds the Latinity of the more recent Pontifex Maximus.

SIXTVS V. PONT. MAX.

OBELISCVM HVNC

A CAESARE AVG. SOLI

IN CIRCO MAXIMO RITV

DICATVM IMPIO

MISERANDA RVINA

FRACTVM OBRVTVMQ.

ERVI TRANSFERRI

FORMAE SVAE REDDI

CRVCIQ. INVICTISS.

DEDICARI IVSSIT

AN. M.D.LXXXIX. PONT. IIII.

ANTE SAGRAM

ILLIVS AEDEM

AVGVSTIOR

LAETIORQ. SURGO

CVIVS EX VTERO

VIRGINALI

AVG. IMPERANTE

SOL IVSTITIAE

EXORTVS EST.[1]

The material of the obelisk is of red granite, and the height of its shaft, without base or ornament, is 78 ft. 6 in., the entire height of the monument from the ground to the top of the cross being 112 ft.[2] The hieroglyphics, according to a translation made by Rev. G. Tomlinson in 1841, read as follows,

[1] Parker, *Obelisks of Rome*, p. 7.

[2] According to Murray's *Rome*. Bonomi's measurements are a trifle less, and he indicates that a portion of the true base being broken off, its actual dimensions are uncertain.

taking the centre lines which refer to Seti I. first,
before those added by his vain-glorious son : [1]

Centre Column, East Side.

" The Horus, the powerful, beloved of justice,
King Pharaoh, guardian of justice, approved of the
sun,
Amen-Mai Rameses,
He erected edifices like the stars of heaven,
He has made his deeds to resound above the
heaven,
Scattering the rays of the sun, rejoicing over them
in his house of millions of years.
In the . . . . year of His Majesty,
He has made good this edifice of his father, whom
he loved,
Giving stability to his name in the abode of the sun.
He who has done this is the son of the sun,
Amen-Mai Rameses,
The beloved of Tum, Lord of Heliopolis, giving
life for ever."

Centre Column, North Side.

" The Horus, the powerful,
Sanctified by truth,[2]
Lord of diadems, Lord of upper and lower Egypt,
Month[3] of the world, possessor(?) of Egypt,
The resplendent Horus, the Osiris(?), the divine
priest of Totanen,
The king, Pharaoh, the establisher of justice,
Who renders illustrious the everlasting edifices of
Heliopolis,
By foundations (fit) for the support of the heaven,

[1] "On the Flaminian Obelisk," with a plate by Joseph Bonomi, in *Trans. Roy. Soc. Lit.*, Vol. I., New Series, p. 176.

[2] Or justice.

[3] An allusion to the sun god Mentu or Month, who was particularly favourable to Rameses II. at the second battle of Kadesh.

Who has established, honoured, and adorned the
temple of the sun,
And of the rest of the gods,
Which have been sanctified by him, the son of the
sun,
Menephtha-Sethai, the beloved of the spirits of
Heliopolis,[1]
Eternal like the sun."

Centre Column, South Side.

" The Horus, the powerful,
The piercer of foreign countries by his victories ;
The Lord of diadems, Lord of upper and lower
Egypt,
The establisher of everlasting edifices;
The resplendent Horus,
Making his sanctuary in the sun who loves him;
The king, Pharaoh, establisher of justice,
The adorner of Heliopolis,
Who makes libations to the sun,
And the rest of the Lords of the heavenly world,
Who gives delight by his rejoicings and by his
eyes.
He does it, the son of the sun, Menephtha-Sethai,
Beloved of Horus, the Lord of the two worlds,
Like the sun, everlasting."

Centre Column, West Side.

" The Horus, the powerful,
The beloved of the sun and of justice,
Lord of diadems, Lord of upper and lower Egypt,
Source of foreign countries, piercer of the Shep-
herds,[2]
The resplendent Horus,
Beloved of the sun, whose name is magnified ;

---

[1] The spirits or local deities were sometimes represented as birds, a
species of bennu, or phœnix, but the translation is obscure.

[2] Doubtful translation, probably "smiter of the Asiatics."

The king, Pharaoh, establisher of justice,
Who fills Heliopolis with obelisks,
To illustrate with (their) rays the temple of the sun;
Who, like the phœnix,[1]
Fills with good things the great temple of the gods,
Inundating(?) it with rejoicings.
He does it, who is the son of the sun,
Menephtha-Sethai, beloved of the rest of the gods
Who inhabit the great temple giving life."

East Side, Right Column.

" The Horus, the powerful,
The beloved of the sun, the Ra,
The offspring of the gods, the subjugator of the
    world,
The king, the Pharaoh, guardian of justice,
Approved of the sun, son of the sun,
Amen-Mai Rameses,
Who gives joy to the region of Heliopolis,
When it beholds the radiance of the solar mountain.
He who does this is the Lord of the world,
The Pharaoh, guardian of justice,
Approved of the sun, son of the sun,
Amen-Mai Rameses, giving life like the sun."

East Side, Left Column.

" The Horus, the powerful, the beloved of justice,
The resplendent Horus,
The director of the years, the great one of victories,
The king, Pharaoh, guardian of justice,
Approved of the sun, son of the sun,
Amen-Mai Rameses, has adorned
Heliopolis with great edifices, honouring the gods
By (placing) their statues in the great temple.
He, the Lord of the world,
Pharaoh, guardian of justice,

---

[1] Doubtful translation.

Approved of the sun, son of the sun,
Amen-Mai Rameses, giving life for ever."

North Side, Right Column.

" The Horus, the powerful, the beloved of the sun,
The Ra, begotten of the gods,
The subjugator of the world,
The king, Pharaoh, approved of the sun,
Son of the sun, Amen-Mai Rameses,
Who magnifies his name in every region
By the greatness of his victories,
The Lord of the world,
Pharaoh, guardian of justice,
Approved of the sun, son of the sun,
Amen-Mai Rameses, giving life like the sun."

North Side, Left Column.

" The Horus, the powerful, the son of Set,[1]
The resplendent Horus,
The director of the years, the great one of victories,
The king, Pharaoh, the guardian of justice,
Approved of the sun, son of the son,
Amen-Mai Rameses,
Who fills the temple of the phœnix with splendid
    objects,
The Lord of the world, Pharaoh, the guardian of
    justice,
Approved of the sun, the son of the sun,
Amen-Mai Rameses, giving life for ever."

South Side, Left Column.

" The Horus, the powerful, the beloved of justice,
Lord of the panegyries,
Like his father Ptah-Totanen; the king,
Pharaoh, guardian of justice, approved of the sun,
Son of the sun, Amen-Mai Rameses,

[1] Rather, descendant of Set-i-pet-i-Nubti, the first of the shepherd kings, who was named after his local deity.

Begotten and educated by the gods,
Builder of their temples, Lord of the world ;
Pharaoh, guardian of justice, approved of the sun,
son of the sun,
Amen-Mai Rameses, giving life like the sun."

South Side, Second Left Column.

" The Horus, the powerful, the son of Ptah-Totonen,
Lord of diadems, Lord of upper and lower Egypt,
Possessor of Egypt, chastiser of foreign countries,
The king, Pharaoh, guardian of justice,
Approved of the sun, son of the sun,
Amen-Mai Rameses, who causes rejoicing in
Heliopolis
By displaying his royal attributes,
Lord of the world, Pharaoh, guardian of justice,
Approved of the sun, son of the sun,
Amen-Mai Rameses, giving life for ever."

West Side, Left Column.

" The Horus, the powerful, the beloved of the sun,
Lord of the panegyries, like his father Ptah-
Totanen,
The king, Pharaoh, guardian of justice,
Approved of the sun, son of the sun, Amen-Mai
Rameses,
Lord of diadems, possessor of Egypt,
Chastiser of foreign countries, Lord of the world ;
Pharaoh, guardian of justice, approved of the sun,
son of the sun,
Amen-Mai Rameses, son of Totanen, giving life."

Right Column, West Side.

" The Horus, the powerful, the son of Tum,
The Ra, offspring of the gods, subjugator of the
world ;
The king, Pharaoh, guardian of justice, approved
of the sun,

The son of the sun, Amen-Mai Rameses,
The resplendent Horus, the director of the years,
The great one of victories, the Lord of the world ;
Pharaoh, guardian of justice, approved of the sun,
   the son of the sun,
Amen-Mai Rameses, the son of Totanen, eternal."

Thus much for the self-laudation of the Egyptian Pharaohs.

This is, according to some writers, the obelisk which was said to have been anciently translated by Hermapion ; other writers, however, consider that of the Lateran to have furnished his text ; most probably, as Champollion[1] states, the translation of Hermapion is only a general statement of the nature of obelisk inscriptions, as none of those now in Rome agree with the Greek priest's version on all points.

CHAPTER XIV.

The Translation of Hermapion.

WHEN Constantine the Great revived the use of the obelisk as an architectural embellishment in the cities of Alexandria, and, as he intended, also, of Rome, the real symbolism of the monolith had not only been long forgotten, but the language in which its in-scriptions were written had become a forgotten tongue, and the purport of its strangely pictorial sentences im-perfectly remembered by vague tradition. Christianity had pronounced against the arts of Egypt as being in themselves wicked and magical, and of all these arts the most important, because in it were concentrated the secrets of them all, was the hieroglyphic writing.

[1] Champollion, *Precis.*

The action of the first Christian Emperor in once more erecting an obelisk excited a passing interest in the nature of the records contained upon it, and accordingly an Egypto-Grecian priest named Hermapion, of whom nothing besides his name is known,[1] gave to the clergy what he professed was a translation of the hieroglyphics of the obelisk in the Circus Maximus. This translation, the first attempt which was ever made to render intelligible the language of the Pharaohs, has been preserved for posterity by the historian Ammianus Marcellinus.[2] That the general sense of Hermapion's rendering is accurate there is no reason to doubt, but the researches of Champollion and Lepsius have since proved that it is not taken from a transcript of the characters of any obelisk now existing at Rome. There are, of course, certain phrases which resemble those occurring again and again on the obelisks of the Lateran and the Porta del Popolo, but there the resemblance ceases, and it is evident that the Egyptian priest in his anxiety to please his masters, either professed a knowledge which he had not, or else altered the phraseology of his text to suit their prejudices and his own. Still it is a point worthy of notice, that from the period of Hermapion all knowledge even of the meanings of a few characters of the Egyptian syllabaries passes away, and the curse of silence punished the prejudices of bigotry till fourteen centuries had elapsed, and the petrified invocations of Rameses to his father Ra were again rendered audible in our ears by the instinctive penetration of Champollion. The following is the translation of Hermapion,[3] in which Helios represents Ra throughout:

[1] Sharpe, *Egypt under the Romans*, p. 147.

[2] Ammian. Marcell. in Long's *Egypt. Antiq.*, I., 338.

[3] Hermapion was probably originally named after the gods Thoth and Apis. The first-named deity being always by the Greek writers called Hermes.

" This says Helios (the sun) to king Rhamestes;[1]
We have given to thee all the world to reign over
    with joy,
Thee whom Helios loves and Apollo :
The strong truth-loving son of Heron,
Born of the gods, the founder ($\kappa\tau\iota\sigma\tau\eta s$) of the world
Whom Helios has chosen, strong in war, king
    Rhamestes,
To whom the whole earth is subdued
With strength and courage :
King Rhamestes of eternal life."

Second Inscription.

" Apollo the strong, he who stands upon truth,
The Lord of the diadem, who possesses Egypt
    in glory,
Who has adorned the city of the sun,
And founded ($\kappa\tau\iota\sigma\alpha s$) the rest of the world,
And has greatly honoured the gods established in
    the city of Helios ,
Whom Helios loves."

Third Inscription.

" Apollo[2] the mighty, the blazing son of Helios,
Whom Helios has chosen, and Ares[3] the valiant has
    favoured ;
Whose good things last for ever, whom Ammon
    loves ;
Who fills the temple of the Phoenix with good
    things,
To whom the gods have given length of life ;
Apollo the mighty, the son of Heron,
To Rhamestes the king of the world,
Who has protected Egypt by conquering foreigners;
Whom Helios loves, to whom the gods have given
    long life,
The Lord of the world, Rhamestes of eternal life."

[1] Rameses II.   [2] Har-em-akhu.   [3] Mentu or Month.

Fourth Inscription.

" Helios, the great god, the Lord of the heaven,
I have given to thee life free from sorrow,
Apollo the mighty, the Lord of the diadem, the in-
comparable,
To whom the Lord of Egypt has erected statues in
this royal town,
And has adorned the city of Helios,'
And Helios himself, the Lord of the heavens.
He has completed his noble work,
The son of Helios, the everliving king."

Fifth Inscription.

" Helios, the Lord of the heavens :
To king Rhamestes have I given might and power;
Whom Apollo loves, the Lord of the times,
Whom Hephæstus² the father of the gods has
chosen through Ares,
The noble king ; the son of Helios, by Helios
beloved."

Sixth Inscription.

" The great god of the city of Helios,
The heavenly, Apollo the mighty, the son of Heron,(?)
Whom Helios loves, whom the gods honour,
Who rules the whole earth, whom Helios chose,
The king mighty through Ares, whom Ammon loves;
And the bright burning king for ever."

CHAPTER XV.

The Obelisk of Trinita dei Monte.

THIS is one of the smaller of the Egyptian
obelisks, being only 48 ft. high,³ excluding the

¹ Heliopolis.   ² Ptah-Totanen.
³ According to Bonomi, it is only 43 ft. 6 in. in height.

base, by 4 ft. 3 in. in diameter; its apex is plain, and each of its four faces has three lines of hieroglyphics: the central one, as usual, referring to the acts of Seti I., and the two outer columns to those of his son, Rameses II. The material in which it is constructed is red granite, and from the style of art in which the characters are cut, it is the general opinion of antiquaries that the monument is an ancient Roman copy of the larger obelisk in Piazza del Popolo. It originally stood in the centre of the Circus of Sallust, and like all of its companion monoliths, was overthrown at the fall of Rome. The art-loving Pontiff, Pius VI., to whose energies and taste the Eternal City will for centuries bear witness, employed the architect Antinori to erect this obelisk, supplying it with an appropriate base, and the orthodox Christian finials. This was done in A.D. 1789, and the Quirinal Mount, upon which the Church of La Trinita dei Monte is situated, received again the honour which it formerly derived from conquered Egypt and pagan Rome. The text upon it has not yet been translated.

CHAPTER XVI.

Obelisks of Rameses II.

AFTER Seti-Menepthah, the next Egyptian monarch who distinguished himself by the erection of obelisks, as well as temples, was his son Rameses II., who took as his surname the title of Meri-Amen, "Beloved of Amen," by which he is best known in history. In order to please the dominant clergy he was associated with his father on the throne of Egypt when only ten years old, and became sole king at the age of eighteen or twenty. Like Seti I., Rameses was attached to the worship of the Syrian god Set, and erected a small temple at Karnak in his honour ; a temple, the inscriptions in which were afterwards effaced as the monarch from motives of policy, or conviction, became more orthodox. He was as great a warrior as his father, and even a still greater builder of temples and palaces, chiefly of the temples of Ipsambul, the Ramessium, Memphis, Karnak, Luxor, Abydos, and Tanis. He further caused to be constructed a colossal statue representing himself at the city of Memphis. On these various monuments his name in the cartouches is found written in as many as thirty different ways. Warlike from his youth, his first engagements were against the Ethiopians, whom he completely overcame; but his chief wars took place with the Khitæ, or Hittites, in a battle where, by his extreme hardihood he nearly lost his life in an ambush set by his foes, from which he was only delivered by his own bravery and that of his armour-bearer Menna. Ultimately Rameses concluded a treaty of peace with Khitasira, the king of the Hittites, and took his daughter to wife, giving her the Egyptian name of Ra-maa-ur-nefru, " The Most Beautiful Sun." He invaded Palestine and took the fortress of Shaluma or Shalem, the Jerusalem of Hebrew history ; and besides many other fortresses he built those of Pakhalem and Raameses, which have been identified with the treasure cities Pithom and Rameses of the Bible, in which case he must have been the Pharaoh of the Exodus. Rameses II. also continued a wall which was begun by his father Seti, from Pelusium to Heliopolis, as a defence to the kingdom against the Asiatics. He married many times, and one of his daughters named Bentanath, became a queen, but of what country it is not known. Equally fond of singularity as of display Rameses was generally accompanied in battle by a favourite lion and dog.

He reigned alone for sixty-seven years, and was buried, not as was usual among the kings of Egypt, but in one of the chambers of the Serapeum or burial place of the divine bull, Apis, at Memphis. His successor was Menepthah II., his thirteenth son; all his other sons having died before him. One of his surnames, Setesura, was the origin of the royal name Sesostris of the Greeks. He is doubtfully said to have had 166 children, 59 of them being sons; and by one Egyptologist, to have married his own daughter, the queen Bentanath.[1]

The chief obelisks set up by Rameses II. were those at Luxor, one of which still maintains its ancient position; the other, the westernmost, having fallen down, was removed to Paris by the French army, and now forms the chief attraction of the noble Place de la Concorde in that beautiful city. The obelisk of Luxor is, like all true obelisks, wrought in fine red granite; it stands, without including its pedestal, about 82 ft. high by 8 ft. in diameter; the apex, having been originally covered by a metal cap, is not sculptured, and has been much eroded, if indeed it was not intentionally left in a rough condition; each of the four faces of the obelisk contains three vertical lines of deeply cut hieroglyphs in honour of Rameses II., the hieroglyphics on this obelisk being particularly deeply cut and well formed. There is a peculiarity in the lines of this monument which could only be noticed when it and its companion obelisk were standing together, this peculiarity consisted in a sensible curvation of the two interior faces of the monoliths, which according to Sir Gardner Wilkinson was designed to obviate the shadow thrown by the sun on a plane surface. " The exterior angle thus formed by the intersecting lines of direction of either side of the face is about three degrees; and

---

[1] *Archaic Dictionary*, Rameses II.

this is one of the many proofs of their (the Egyptians')
attentive observation of the phenomena of nature."[1]

The bases of the Obelisk of Luxor are adorned
with sculptures upon each of their four faces ; the
north and south sides having figures in high relief
of the sacred cynocephelus ape (*aani*) 🐒, standing
in an attitude of adoration, as they are frequently
represented on the mystical papyri when worshipping
the sun, Tum, in the underworld ; the eastern and
western faces of the bases have standing figures of
the god Nilus, or Hapimou, bringing offerings; these
are carved in the sharp, low, *incavo relievo*, peculiar
to Egyptian art.[2] The bases rested upon two low
steps of limestone.

To an Egyptian whose delighted eyes beheld
Luxor in all its glory at the close of the XIXth
dynasty, the effect presented by the position and
environments of these two obelisks must have been
fine in the extreme. Behind them rose the stupendous pylons adorned with flag staves, and between
the temple and the bases of the obelisks were two
colossal statues of Rameses himself, crowned with
the sacred crown of the united kingdom, holding in
his hands the mysterious symbol of life, and sitting
in that solemn attitude of placid power which was
assumed by the gods and the Pharaohs their co-.
equals ; in front of these statues and obelisks a
long avenue of ram-headed sphinxes, a portion of that
stately dromos which connected this temple with
that at Karnak, extended for a distance of nearly
two miles, passing through a verdant district flanked
with smaller temples and adorned by gigantic
statues and sculptured colonnades. Taking the
two great temples of Thebes, Luxor and Karnak
together, the nations of the world probably never
produced a more imposing or more costly series of

---

[1] Murray, *Egypt*, p. 374.   [2] Wilkinson's *Thebes*, p. 350.

palace shrines. Had not an earthquake in recent times aided by its spasmodic fury the malicious wrath of men, Luxor and Karnak with their obelisks and colossi would have continued to this day, as strong and nearly as perfect as when Rameses II. was carried on the shoulders of his officers through ranks of adoring slaves, to signify his approbation of the works constructed in his name and designed to perpetuate his glory.

—————

CHAPTER XVII.

The Obelisk of Paris.

WHEN the victorious quasi-scientific armies of Napoleon entered Egypt, they opened to the literati and antiquarians of Europe the sealed treasures of the south, and stimulated an interest in the monuments of Egypt among the capitals of the west, which had not been excited for more than a century before; indeed, not since the publication by Pocock, and Corneille Le Brun, of their respective travels in Egypt, and the Holy Land.[1] The intention of Napoleon was to have carried off from upper Egypt the most striking objects of ancient art, but the genius of Sir Ralph Abercrombie terminated his successes in Egypt; and the bravery of Nelson, and

[1] Pocock's *Travels* contain the first accurate accounts of many of the Egyptian temples, together with drawings of the vocal Memnon, the Egyptian tombs, and the Sinaitic inscriptions. The work was, as usual in those days, published by subscription, and the plates separately paid for by individual donors, chiefly College friends of the author, and, in consequence, the best skill of the engraver has often been devoted to the delineation of their armorial bearings at the foot of the plates; a subject which he was evidently more familiar with than antiquities.

Le Brun's *Voyages* chiefly deal with Arabia, Palestine, and the East. The plates are still less reliable than Pocock's.

the capitulation of Alexandria, threw into the hands
of the English the sculptures that the French had
marked for themselves. Of these monuments the
greatest was the fallen obelisk at Luxor; but with the
indifference to art which has generally marked a
popular ministry, the government of Pitt took no
steps to secure either that or the prostrate obelisk at
Alexandria, which was also offered to it; and the
principal relic carried away as a military trophy was
the Rosetta Stone, more on account of its portability
than its apparent value, which has since proved to be
inestimable. Circumstances did not allow, for many
years, either England or France to turn their attention
from the present to the past, but in 1831 Mehemet Ali
offered to the British and the French the obelisks of
Alexandria, even proposing to defray the transport
of the fallen obelisk to the deck of the English ship
at his own expense. Unwisely prudent, the State declined the offer, but the French Government more
cautiously sent out Champollion Le Jeune, the famous
Egyptologist and jointly with Dr.Young, the discoverer
of the language of the Pharaohs, to examine and report
upon the whole question. Champollion, therefore,
made a thorough examination of all the obelisks
in the country, and ultimately reported in favour
of those at Luxor. Upon the ministers of Louis
Philippe accepting his decision, the Viceroy of Egypt
allowed the removal of the westernmost of the two
obelisks of Rameses II.; and on the part of the
French a vessel especially designed for the transport
of the monolith was built at Toulon, for the purpose
of conveying it to Europe, and it sailed under the
conduct of Lieut. Verninac St. Maur in 1831, who on
his return wrote an interesting account of the whole expedition.[1] The *Louqsor*, for so was the vessel named,
arrived at Luxor in the heat of the summer, and
M. De St. Maur and the engineer Lebas, a pupil of

[1] *Voyage du Luxor en Egypte*, 1835.

l'Ecole Polytechnique, at once cleared out the bases
of both obelisks, when it was discovered that, owing
to the westernmost one being a little the shorter, the
pedestals were of unequal height, and one a little
in advance of the other. A considerable time was
spent in Egypt in dislodging, packing, and removing the smaller obelisk ; and upon its being
taken down it was ascertained that it had been
originally cracked and mended again by two dove-
tailed wedges of wood before it was placed in position
by Rameses II. ; these wedges had, however, completely perished by the moisture which had crept in
and condensed between the base and the plinth of the
obelisk. With so much deliberation and trouble was
the transport of the obelisk effected, that it was not
landed at Paris till December 23, 1833. Equal care
was taken with its re-erection in the Place de la
Concorde. A long inclined plane of wood and earth
was made, reaching from the vessel in which it lay to
the base upon which the monument was to be set up;
and it was finally re-elevated without injury or risk
on October 25, 1836, "*aux applaudissements d'un
peuple immense.*"[1]   In the open circus in which it
stands, unimpeded by narrow streets, and undis-
figured by the gilded ornamentations which are added
to the obelisk of Rome, this obelisk marks at one and
the same time the majesty of ancient Egypt, and the
power of modern France.[2]   In its dimensions the
obelisk of Paris is a little shorter than that at Luxor:
being, according to Bonomi, 76 ft. 6 in. in height by
8 ft. wide at the base. The apex is left unfinished,

[1] See Delaborde, *Précis des Operations relatives au Transport d'un de ces
Monumens dans la Capitale*, 1832.
[2] A full and most interesting account of the difficulties attending the
transit of this obelisk, is given by M. De St. Maur himself, in *La Voyage
du Louqsor*, 1835. The construction of a ship to carry away the monument was a revival of the method adopted by Constantius, A.D. 357, when
he transported to Rome the obelisk of the Lateran; which latter was conveyed along the Mediterranean in a galley steered by 300 rowers.

and still seems to demand in the damp air of Europe
the protection of its former gilded cap.   The following is a translation by M. Chabas of the hieroglyphics
which cover its four sides.[1]

North Side, Central Column.

" The Horus-sun, strong bull of the sun,
  Who has smitten the barbarian,
  Lord of the diadems,
  Who fights millions, magnanimous lion, golden hawk,
  Strongest in all the world
  Ousor-ma-Ra,[2] bull at his limit,
  Obliging the whole earth to come before him.
  By the will of Amen his august father
  He has made the obelisk,
  The son of the sun, Mei-Amen-Rameses, living
    eternally."

North Side, Left Column.

" The Horus-sun, strong bull, the strongest (of the
    strongest)
  Who fights with his sword,
  King of great roarings, master of terror,
  Whose valour strikes the whole earth,
  King of upper and lower Egypt,
  Ousor-ma-Ra, Sotep-en-Ra, son of the sun, Mei-
    Amen-Rameses,
  Whose dominion is twice cherished
  Like that of the god inhabiting Thebes,
  King of upper and lower Egypt,
  Ousor-ma-Ra, Sotep en-Ra,
  Son of the sun, Mei-Amen-Rameses, the **vivifier**."

North Side, Right Column.

" The Horus-sun, strong bull, the Lord of the tria-
    contacride festivals,

[1] Published in *Records of the Past*, Vol. IV., p. 17.
[2] Prenomen of Rameses II.

Who loves the two worlds, king strong by his sword,
Who hath seized both worlds,
Supreme chief whose royalty is great as that of the
   god Tum,
King of upper and lower Egypt,
Ousor-ma-Ra, Sotep-en-Ra, Mei-Amen-Rameses,
The chiefs of the entire world are under his feet;
King of upper and lower Egypt,
Ousor-ma-Ra, Sotep-en-Ra,
Son of the sun, Mei-Amen-Rameses, vivifier."

East Side, Central Column.

" The Horus-sun, strong bull, fighting with his sword,
   Lord of the diadems, who subdues[1] whoever
   approaches him,
Who seizes the ends of the world,
Golden hawk, very terrible, master of valour,
King of upper and lower Egypt,
Ousor-ma-Ra,
Divine issue of his father Amen, Lord of gods.
Causing to be joyous the temple of the soul,
And the gods of the great temple in joy.
He has made the obelisk,
The son of the sun, Mei-Amen-Rameses, living
   eternally."

East Side, Left Column.

" The Horus-sun, strong bull, son of Amen,
How multiplied are his monuments!
The very strong, beloved son of the sun on his throne,
King of upper and lower Egypt,
Ousor-ma-Ra, Sotep-en-Ra, son of the sun,
Mei-Amen-Rameses, who has erected the dwelling
   of Amen [2]
Like the heavenly horizon, by his great monuments
   for eternity.
King of upper and lower Egypt,
Son of the sun, Mei-Amen-Rameses, vivifier."

---

[1] Strikes down.   [2] Thebes.

East Side, Right Column.

" The Horus, strong bull, beloved of the goddess
   Truth,
King doubly cherished as the god Tum,
Supreme Chief, delight of Amen-Ra for centuries;
King of upper and lower Egypt, Ousor-ma-Ra,
   Sotep-en-Ra,
Son of the sun, Mei-Amen-Rameses ;
As is heaven, that (such) is thy monument ;
Thy name will be permanent like the heavens.
King of upper and lower Egypt, Ousor-ma-Ra,
   Sotep-en-Ra,
Son of the sun Mei-Amen-Rameses, vivifier."

Middle Column, West Side.

" The Horus sun, strong bull, beloved of the goddess
   truth,
Lord of the diadems, who takes care of Egypt and
   chastises nations,
Golden hawk, master of armies, the very strong,
The king of upper and lower Egypt, Ousor-ma-Ra,
King of kings, issue of Tum, one in body with him
To perform his royalty on earth for centuries,
And to render Amen's dwelling happy by the bene-
   factions.
He has made (the obelisk),
The son of the sun, Mei-Amen-Rameses living
   eternally."

Left Column, West Side.

" The Horus sun, strong bull, rich in valour,
King, potent by the sword,
Who has made himself master of the whole world
By his strength, king of upper and lower Egypt,
Ousor-ma-Ra Sotep-en-Ra, son of the sun,
Mei-Amen-Rameses : all countries of the earth
   come to him with their tributes,

King of upper and lower Egypt, Ousor-ma-Ra
Sotep-en-Ra,
Son of the sun, Mei-Amen-Rameses, vivifier."

Right Column, West Side.

" The Horus sun, strong bull, beloved of the sun,
King who is a great plague (to his enemies);
The whole earth trembles in terror of him,
King of upper and lower Egypt, Ousor-ma-Ra-
Sotep-en-Ra,
Son of the sun (Mei-Amen Rameses),
Son of Mont, whom Mont has formed with his
hand,[1]
King of upper and lower Egypt, Ousor-ma-Ra-
Sotep-en-Ra,
Son of the sun, Mei-Amen-Rameses, vivifier."

Middle Column, South Side.

" The Horus sun, strong bull, very valorous,
King of upper and lower Egypt,
Ousor-ma-Ra Sotep-en-Ra, eldest son of the king
of the gods,
Who has raised him on his throne on the earth,
Like an only lord; possessor of the whole
world ;
He knows him, as he (the king) had done homage
to him
By bringing to perfection his dwelling for millions
of years,
Mark of the preference he had in the Southern Ap
for his father,[2]
Who will prefer him for millions of years.
He has made (the obelisk),
The son of the sun, Mei-Amen-Rameses, vivifier,
eternal as the sun."

[1] The hostile or warlike form of the sun god **Ra**.
[2] A district of Thebes.

Left Column, South Side.

"The Horus sun, strong bull, loved by the goddess
Truth,
King of upper and lower Egypt,
Ousor-ma-Ra Sotep-en-Ra,
Son of the sun, Mei-Amen-Rameses, descendant of
the sun,
Protected by Harmachis, illustrious seed, precious
egg of the sacred eye,[1]
Emanation of the king of the gods, to be the
only lord,
Possessor of the whole world,
King of upper and lower Egypt,
Ousor-ma-Ra Sotep-en-Ra,
Son of the sun, Mei-Amen-Rameses, eternal vivi-
fier."

Right Column, South Side.

"The Horus sun, strong bull, beloved of the sun.
King of upper and lower Egypt,
Ousor-ma-Ra Sotep-en-Ra, son of the sun,
Mei-Amen-Rameses, king, excellent, warlike,
Vigilant to seek the favours of him who has be-
gotten him ;
Thy name is permanent as the heavens ;
The length of thy life is like the solar disk therein
(the heaven),
King of upper and lower Egypt,
Ousor-ma-Ra Sotep-en-Ra,
Son of the sun, Mei-Amen-Rameses, eternal vivi-
fier like the sun."

THE OBELISKS OF SAN.

When the Hykshos ruled in Egypt one of the chief
cities which they conquered and adapted to themselves was the town of San, a town originally founded

[1] An allusion to the divine eye. The sun and moon being the sacred
eyes of deity, and the god Khnum the spirit, the egg, or pupil of those eyes.

in the north-west of the Delta by the monarchs of the XIIth dynasty. Expelling from its walls all the resident Egyptians, and destroying all the temples and palaces which they could not adapt to the purposes of their own worship, the Shepherds rebuilt the city as one peculiarly their own, and introduced into its sculpture and architecture their strongly Asiatic style of art. When the restoration of the ancient regime, and consequently their own expulsion, took place under the first kings of the XVIIIth dynasty, San was one of the first places in which the Hykshos were attacked, and one of the last from which they were expelled. Hence the Egyptians considering the whole place as entirely defiled, con-tented themselves with destroying the buildings of the hated Asiatics, and delivering the captured town to desolation. In the XIXth dynasty, however, Rameses II., who it has been already observed was more than half of Hykshos descent and faith, deter-mined to restore the former capital, and therefore re-founded the original temples, dedicating afresh others to Ra, Tum, and Horus, all solar deities, together with Sutekh the Semitic god. The edifices of Rameses II. at San were particularly splendid and uniform in their design, and as they were chiefly connected with the worship of Ra, so there was a larger number of obelisks than was usually erected at one time by the same monarch. In the ruins of San, or Tanis as the city was afterwards called,[1] no less than ten obelisks bearing the cartouch of Rameses II. have been discovered; these are generally broken, and they appear to have formed a grand avenue in front of the temple of Ra. The heights of the obelisks vary ;

[1] San, or Tanis was again the capital of lower Egypt under the XXIInd and XXIIIrd dynasties; but the Pharaohs of the XXVIth dynasty gave a fatal blow to its importance, by removing the seat of government to Sais. Under the Greek dominion it was plundered of its monuments by the Ptolemies, and it finally perished as a city of any note under the Edict of Theodosius, A.D. 379.

some when entire may have been 50 or 60 ft. high,
with a mean diameter of 5 ft. ; others, chiefly at
the lower end of the avenue, measure about 33 ft.
in altitude ; they also vary as to the amount of inscription upon them, some having one and others two
vertical lines of hieroglyphics; all of them are, however, still prostrate, though it would be an enterprise
deserving the notice of European lovers of art, to
remove one or two of them to one of the cities of
Europe, and re-establish it to the admiration of mankind. Who will be the Erasmus Wilson of Dublin,
Edinburgh, or Glasgow ?

CHAPTER XVIII.

Other Obelisks of Rameses II.

FACING the still stately and almost perfect
Rotunda, or Pantheon, which was erected by
Agrippa twenty years before the Christian era, and
which has never since its consecration ceased to be
a place of prayer, stands the upper portion of what
was once a fine obelisk of Rameses II., and still,
albeit but a fragment, of nearly 20 ft. in height.[1]
Although the work of the Egyptian sculptors of the
XIXth dynasty, yet, inasmuch as, like that of the
Piazza della Minerva it bears also the cartouch of
Psametik II., it has been attributed to that later
monarch. The obelisk is of red granite, and has but
a single column of hieroglyphics, with the cartouch
of Rameses II. on each of the four sides. According
to some writers[2] it is conjectured to have formed
one of a pair of obelisks which were carried away

[1] According to Murray's *Rome* it is only 17 feet high.
[2] Murray's *Rome*, 284.

from Egypt by one of the later emperors, and then set up afresh in front of the temple of Isis and Serapis in the Campus Martius. The site of that temple was afterwards occupied by the Dominican Convent della Minerva, and the obelisks were re-discovered A.D. 1665. Parker, in his recent work on the Obelisks of Rome, asserts on the contrary, that this obelisk was one (of several) which stood on the Spina of the Circus Maximus, from whence it was removed by Pope Paul V., A.D. 1620, and set up in the Piazza di S. Martini; and that it was trans-ferred to the centre of the fountain which beautifies the Piazza della Rotunda, in the year 1711, by the order of Clement XI.[1]

THE OBELISK OF THE VILLA MATTEI.

The last of the obelisks of Rameses II. which remains to be described is a small one of red granite, about 8 ft. 3 in. high; it was found with the other obelisks of the Minerva and the Rotunda on the site of the ancient temple of Isis, and like them bears also the cartouch of Psametik II. It is much damaged, and was placed in its present site in the gardens of the Villa Mattei, on the Cœlian Mount, by the order of Pope Sixtus V., A.D. 1590.

A rather sad anecdote is attached to this obelisk, for it is related that while it was being raised upon its pedestal, the architect in his anxiety to steady the monument, incautiously placed his hand upon the pedestal at the moment when the cords were relaxed, the ponderous stone at once descended crushing the fingers, and as it was impossible to lift up the mono-lith the architect had to have his hand cut off, leaving the bones of his fingers under the obelisk, where to this day Roman gossip imagines they are still to be seen.[2]

---

[1] Parker, *Obelisks*, p. 9.   [2] *Ibid.*, p. 7.

CHAPTER XIX.

The Obelisks of the Later Dynasties.

HERODOTUS tells us in one of his gossiping historiettes, that when Egypt was parcelled out into a confederacy of twelve petty kingdoms, the monarchs were in the wont of sacrificing at stated intervals in the temple of Vulcan, or more properly Ptah Sokari; and that upon one occasion as they were sacrificing in the temple of Vulcan, and were about to offer a libation on the last day of the festival, "the high-priest, mistaking the number, brought out eleven of the twelve golden bowls with which he used to make the libation, whereupon he who stood last of them, Psammetichus, since he had not a bowl, having taken off his helmet which was of brass, held it out and made the libation ; all the other kings were in the habit of wearing helmets, and at .that time had them on. Psammetichus, therefore, without any sinister intention, held out his helmet; but they having taken into consideration what was done by Psammetichus, and the oracle that had foretold to them that 'whosoever among them should offer a libation from a brazen bowl, should be sole king of Egypt,' calling to mind the oracle, they did not think it right to put him to death, since upon examination they found that he had done it by no premeditated design, but they determined to banish him to the marshes, having divested him of the greatest part of his power; and they forbade him to leave the marshes, or to have any intercourse with the rest of Egypt. Afterwards, having been made king, he was a second time constrained to go into exile among the marshes on account of the helmet. Knowing then, that he had been exceedingly injured by them, he entertained the design of avenging himself on his persecutors, and when he sent into the city of Buto to consult the oracle of Latona (Sekhet), where is the truest oracle that the Egyptians have, an answer came, 'that vengeance should come from the sea, when men of brass should appear.' He however, was very incredulous that men of brass should come to assist him; but when no long time had elapsed, stress of weather compelled some Ionians and Carians, who had sailed out for the purpose of piracy, to bear away into Egypt; and when they had disembarked and were clad in brazen armour, an Egyptian who had never before seen men clad in brass went to the marshes to Psammetichus, and told him that men of brass having arrived from the sea were ravaging the plains ; he perceiving that the oracle was accomplished, treated these Ionians and Carians in a friendly manner, and having promised them great things, persuaded them to join with him, and when he had succeeded in persuading them, he then with the help of such Egyptians as were well affected to him, and with these allies, overcame the other kings."[1]

Thus was Egypt, already subjugated to Assyria, de-nationalized by Greece, for from the time of Psametik Greek art, Greek ideas, and Grecian polity prevailed in lower Egypt, to the ultimate destruction of all true native art. The ancient religion also suffered, for the last revision of the great Ritual of the Dead took place about this period, and many new glosses crept in. Civilizations so opposed as those of the Egyptian and the Hellene could not well fare together ; and from the reign of the kings of the XXVIth dynasty, the life spirit departed from the palaces and the creeds of the Pharaohs, though, like their own beautiful mummies, the form remained perfect when the soul had fled. The Grecianization of Egypt by Psametik, and his rendering the study of that language com-pulsory, drove his subjects into a revolt, and 200,000

[1] *Euterpe*, cli.

of them went into voluntary exile to form a new Egypt in Ethiopia. Psametik, however, held his position steadily ; was a great restorer, if not a correct one, and he reigned for certainly not less than fifty-two years, when he was succeeded by his son, Necho II.

As an obelisk rearer, this crafty usurper is best known by the lofty obelisk which stands in the centre of the Monte Citorio at Rome. It was originally removed from Heliopolis by Augustus, A.D. 30, at the same time when he transferred the obelisks of Seti I. and Rameses II. to ornament the Spina of the Circus Maximus. According to Pliny it was set up to serve as the gnomon of a sun-dial in the Campus Martius. "With this object a stone pavement was laid, the extreme length of which corresponded exactly with the length of the shadow thrown by the obelisk at the sixth hour on the day of the winter solstice.[1] After this period the shadow would go on day by day gradually decreasing ; and then again (after the summer solstice) would as gradually increase, corresponding with certain lines of brass that were inserted in the stone, a device well deserving to be known, and due to the ingenuity of Facundus Novus, the mathematican. Upon the apex of the obelisk he placed a gilded ball, in order that the shadow of the summit might be condensed and agglomerated, and so prevent the shadow of the apex itself from running to a fine point of enormous extent ; the plan being first suggested to him, it is said, by the shadow that is projected by the human head."[2] This obelisk was first discovered, after the fall of Rome, in the ruins beneath the choir of S. Lorenzo in Lucina, in the year 1748, during the Pontificate of Benedict XIV., by the architect Zabaglia. It was not removed, however, till the time of Pius VI., who had it set up again in 1792, repairing it with the fragments of the Aurelian

[1] Or, 12 a.m.   [2] *Hist. Nat.*, Book xxxvi., Chap. 15.

Column which was found near it, and the larger portion of which was employed to form a base for it.
The obelisk was then repaired; and to do this was a
work of some delicacy, inasmuch as the monolith was
broken into four pieces, the lowest of which was so
injured by fire, that it was necessary to substitute a
fresh piece of granite in its place. The hieroglyphics
upon this obelisk are of remarkable beauty of execution. As it now stands, it measures 71 ft. 5 in. in
height, and it has upon each face two lines of hieroglyphics. The pyramidion on the apex is plain: the
material of which it is wrought is the usual red granite
of Syene. The following is the inscription of Augustus
which is engraved upon it, on the east and west sides
of the pedestal :—

IMP. CAESAR. DIVI. F
AVGVSTVS
PONTIFEX. MAXIMVS.
IMP. XII. COS. XI. TRIB. POT. XIV.
AEGYPTO . IN . POTESTATEM
POPVLI . ROMANI . REDACTA
SOLI . DONVM . DEDIT.

"The Imperator Cæsar, son of the deified Julius,
Augustus,
Chief Pontiff,
Imperator for the twelfth time, Consul for the
eleventh, holding tribunitian power for the four-
teenth time,
Upon Egypt being reduced into subjection
To the Roman people,
Presented this obelisk as an offering to the sun." [1]

[1] Murray states this obelisk to have been discovered in the Pontificate of
Julius II., and that it was broken into five fragments. I prefer in this
case to follow the authority of Parker, whose account of the *Obelisks
of Rome* is only just out.

On the other side of the pedestal is engraved :—

PIVS VI. PONT. MAX.
OBELISCVM REGIS SESOSTRIDIS
A C CAESARE AVGVSTO HORARVM
INDICEM IN CAMPO STATVTVM
QVEM IGNIS VI ET TEMPORVM
VETVSTATE CORRVPTVM BENEDICTVS XIV.
P. M. EX AGGESTA HVMO
AMOLITVM RELIQVERAT SQVALORE
DETERSO CVLTVQVE ADDITI VRBI
COELOQVE RESTITVIT
ANNO M.DCCXCII
SACRI PRINCIPATVS EJVS XVIII.

THE OBELISKS OF PSAMETIK II.

This monarch, though the son, was not the im-
mediate successor of his father, Psametik I. He
came to the throne upon the death of Necho II., and
claimed the throne of Ethiopia in addition to that of
Egypt ; and the better to establish his right to it he
married his aunt, the princess Neitaker, the daughter
of queen Shap-en-ap, and the grand-daughter of queen
Amen-iritis, the last of the old royal line. He reigned
with some glory for six years, during which he re-
conquered Ethiopia. The Greeks to whom he was
better known than even to the Egyptians, gave him
the name of Psammis ; and he was succeeded by his
son Uah-pra-het (the sun enlarges his heart), who was
the Hophra of Hebrew history.

THE OBELISK IN THE PIAZZA MINERVA.

This is a small monolith 17 ft. high, of very pale red
granite; and of all the Roman obelisks this has the
greatest inclination of the sides. It bears the cartouch
of Psametik II.; and the Egyptian site for which it was
intended is unknown: possibly it was the city of Sais,
which the Pharaohs of the XXVth dynasty selected

for the capital of their empire. It was found, together
with the obelisk of the Piazza Rotunda, among the
ruins of the temple of Isis and Serapis, where it had
been set up by the Romans. In 1660[1] the architect
Bernini, at the order of Pope Alexander VII., with
very questionable taste, erected the obelisk upon the
back of a marble elephant, the work of Ercole Ferrata;
and his doing so obtained for him from the Roman
populace, the readiest populace in the world to satirise
their notabilities, the surname of "The Elephant."
The obelisk has a plain apex, and but a single line
of hieroglyphics upon each side. Besides its original
fracture it has further suffered considerable injury
since its first re-erection in Rome.

Inscription on the Obelisk of the Piazza della Minerva.

VETEREM OBELISCVM
PALLADIS ÆGYPTIÆ MONVMENTVM
E TELLVRE ERVTVM
ET IN MINERVÆ OLIM
NVNC DEIPARÆ GENETRICIS
FORO ERECTVM
DIVINÆ SAPIENTIÆ ALEXANDER VII.
DEDICAVIT ANNO SALVTIS
MDC.LXVII.

And on the other side of the pedestal.

SAPIENTIS ÆGVPTI
INSCVLPTAS OBELISCO FIGVRAS
AB ELEPHANTO BELLVARVM FOR-
TISSIMA
GESTAS QVISQVIS HIC VIDES
DOCVMENTVM INTELLIGE
ROBVSTÆ MENTIS ESSE
SOLIDAM SAPIENTIAM SVSTINERE.[2]

[1] This is Parker's date for its erection; but, as according to Murray,
the obelisk was only discovered in 1665, there must be an error somewhere.
In another page Parker gives 1667, which is more probably correct.
[2] Parker, *Obelisks of Rome*, p. 8.

8*

THE OBELISKS OF AMYRTÆUS.

In the Egyptian Saloon of the British Museum are two small and mutilated obelisks bearing the cartouch of Amyrtæus I., a petty king of Egypt under the Persian dynasty. His history attests the absolute decline of the Egyptian empire. Aided by Inarus, king of Lybia, he revolted against his master, Artaxerxes, king of Persia, circa B.C. 450, by whom he was after a six-years' struggle subdued and driven into the Delta. Inarus was then impaled, Thannyras placed upon the throne of Lybia, and the Persian vassal chief Pausiris, on that of Egypt.

Brief and turbulent as was the reign of Amyrtæus, it yet enabled him to leave some sculptures bearing his cartouch behind. Of these monuments the two obelisks in the British Museum are the most interesting and peculiar; one of them has been broken in two and reunited: it is 8 ft. 2 in. in height, by a diameter of 1 ft. 6 in. at the base on two of the sides, and nearly 1 ft. 5 in. on the other two;[1] the companion obelisk is about the same dimension, and it has been broken into four pieces; both have lost not only their pyramidions but the upper portion of their summits also. They are, contrary to the symbolical colour of these monuments, wrought in a dark greenish black basalt, and they contain one line of inscription upon each of their four faces. One of these obelisks was first noticed by Pocock as forming part of a window sill in the Castle of Cairo; and the other, broken in two pieces, was discovered by Niebuhr, one fragment serving as the door sill of a mosque in the Castle of Cairo, while a second was the doorstep of a house near Kantara-siedid; he, however, specifies one fragment as being of black marble, and the other of granite, but his illustrations serve to identify the relics with each other. The French

[1] Bonomi, 19 ft. 9 in.   Westropp, *Hand-Book of Archæology*, 17 ft. by 2 ft. 4 in. at the base.

army of occupation carried off these obelisks from Cairo to Alexandria, and they consequently fell into the hands of the English at the capitulation of that city in 1801. Despite the circumstance of their having been often engraved, these monuments have hitherto received less notice than they have deserved on account of the peculiar sharpness of their sculpture, and the natural conventionality of the animal figures delineated in the hieroglyphic signs: a conventionality almost equalling that of the best periods of the art of the XIXth dynasty.[1]

The hieroglyphic inscription has only been partly translated: but that portion so deciphered reads:

"Amyrtæus, the living, like Ra, beloved of Thoth, The great Lord of Eshmunayn."[2]

THE PRIOLI
OBELISK OF CONSTANTINOPLE.

Peter Gyllus, in his *Antiquities of Constantinople*,[3] relates that when he visited Constantinople in the sixteenth century A.D., he noticed, besides the great obelisk in the Hippodrome, a smaller one, which at that time was standing in the Imperial precinct, on the north side of the first hill. "A little time afterwards I saw it lying prostrate without the precinct; and found it to be 35 ft. in length; each of its sides, if I mistake not, was 6 ft. broad, and the whole was 8 yards in compass; it was purchased by Antonio Priolo, a nobleman of Venice, who sent it thither and placed it in St. Stephen's Market." According to Long, this obelisk was never removed, but is identical with one of red granite which still stands in the Sultan's gardens, on the most northern eminence there.[4] From its dimensions this obelisk is probably

[1] Some writers attribute the obelisks to Nectanebo I.

[2] Sharpe, *Egyptian Antiquities*, p. 107; and *Trans. Roy. Soc. Lit.*, Vol. II., Part 2.

[3] Ball's trans. *Gyllus' Antiq. Constantinople*, 1729, p. 104.

[4] Long, *Egypt. Antiq.*, I., p. 332.

of the period of the Middle Empire, but as a copy of its inscriptions has not reached Europe, or been elsewhere published, all speculation as to its original place of erection, or the monarch who erected it, would be useless.

OBELISK OF NAHASB.

At the wells of Nahasb, in the deserts of Arabia Petrea, and consequently beyond the limits of Egypt proper, the traveller Rüppel discovered a small obelisk of sandstone, about 8 ft. long, lying on the ground ; the three sides which were exposed to the atmosphere had lost their sculptures; but the fourth, which from its position was protected, contained hieroglyphics which appeared beautiful, as far as he could examine them.[1] It is to be regretted that no further particulars of this obelisk are known. From its material and size it would seem to have belonged to the Saitic period.

CHAPTER XX.

Ptolemaic and Roman Obelisks.

WITH the accession of the family of Ptolemy Lagus to the throne of the conquered pro- vince of Egypt, a new period of art of architecture takes its rise on the banks of the Nile. The idea of the Egyptian sculpture was still preserved, but the details and the feeling were Roman ; an imperfectly imitated naturalism ill replaced the accurate conven- tionality of the older artist. The affectation of grace often weakened the effect which formerly an honest disregard of anything but true simplicity attained. The Egyptian scribes were, in other words, educated, but not instructed, to perceive for themselves, hence they

[1] Long, *Egyptian Antiquities*, I., p. 323, 324.

could only copy, now no longer from conventional, but from natural objects, tastefully represented, but withal frequently caricatured. Something of this was notice-able in the innovations introduced by the Psammetichi, but the elegant pedantry of the Ptolemaic sovereigns altered and spoiled all. Philopator and Philometor, the two ablest sovereigns of their line, admired Egyptian art, and patronised the Egyptian theology, but it was purely an admiration and a patronage: it was the admiration of a *dilettante* and not of a devotee, and consequently the temples, the pottery, and the paintings of the Greco-Egyptian dynasty are con-spicuously heavy and affected. Architectural details which, while small and properly subordinated were beautiful, became exaggerated into absurd dimensions, and placed in unsuited positions. This was especially the case as regarded the complicated forms of the capitals of the temple columns, which often seemed too weak for the weight they were intended to sustain. Roman ornamentation was combined with Egyptian decoration, and Italian polychromatic design with the more regular harmonic system of Egyptian primary colouration. The famous Cleopatra VI, the murderess of her sister, and the betrayer of her brother and lover, who was, like all of her family, a great temple restorer, completed the degradation of Egyptian architecture, by adapting it wholly to Roman and Greek forms, and producing a series of tasteless structures which only flattery could call beautiful.[1] Of course, copying their nobler and mightier pre-decessors, the Ptolemaic sovereigns erected obelisks to the sun; but these have nearly all perished, or have been used for baser purposes. Some are, however, still known to lie hidden beneath the foundations of Alexandria, and others may be buried in the mud

---

[1] More especially Stadia, Hippodromes, Naumachia Baths, and Libraries, all of which except public libraries were foreign to Egyptian feeling; and for which therefore no really Egyptian plans or details existed.

of the Delta lakes, which covers the site of many Greco-Egyptian cities. The chief obelisks of really Ptolemaic date, as distinct from Roman work, which are now known to exist, are a plain sandstone one at Philæ, the chief buildings of which are Ptolemaic ; and the exquisite little obelisk bearing the name of Ptolemy Alexander I., which is now in the possession of Mr. J. W. Bankes, of Corfe Castle.

In 1815 the enterprising traveller Belzoni, in company with Mr. W. G. Bankes, discovered this obelisk among the ruins of the temple of Philæ, and he at once offered to sell it to his companion, and to remove it to the seashore. His attempts to carry off the monument excited the animosity and opposition of M. Drovetti, an Italian antiquary, who was also on the search for antiquities ; and some very disgraceful manœuvres took place, the history of which was indignantly given by Belzoni in a pamphlet published in London several years later. Every kind of obstacle was placed in the way of Belzoni, and nothing but his indomitable will and great personal strength (he had formerly obtained a living in London as a juggler in feats of strength), could have overcome the difficulties he encountered. On getting the monolith to the water's edge, its great weight broke down the pier, and it slipped into the river. Undisheartened by this want of success, he waited till the fall of the Nile, rolled the obelisk safely to the shore, and ultimately floated it uninjured over the cataracts of Assoun to the port of Alexandria, where he delivered it, together with the sandstone pedestal upon which it had stood, to his employer Mr. Bankes, by whom it was afterwards carried to England, and set up in the gardens in front of his residence, Kingston Hall, Dorset.[1]

The obelisk is of the usual red granite, and is very perfect ; it is 22 ft. in height, by a diameter of 2 ft.

[1] See Belzoni, *Narrative of Operations in Egypt and Nubia*, p. 105, *et seq.*

2 in. at the base ; it has a line of well-cut hieroglyphics down the centre of each face. The inscription is chiefly in honour of Ptolemy Euergetes II., or Alexander I.,[1] and his mother Cleopatra Cocce, and his sister and wife Cleopatra. The base of the monument is of sandstone, and is about 5 ft. high ; it bears a long inscription in Greek, relating to the gods Euergetes, Ptolemy, and the two queens Cleopatra, and to the benefaction of the late Ptolemy Physcon, to the temples and clergy of Philæ. Above the inscription, which was really a petition of the Egyptian priests, are the remains of the royal answer to their requests, an answer which was originally written in letters of gold ; little more than half of the answer remains, but what still exists has been restored by M. Letronne.[2] The whole of the inscriptions, together with the royal reply to the governor Lochus, are as follows :

ΒΑΣΙΛΕΙΠΤΟΛΕΜΑΙΩΙΚΑΙΒΑΣΙΛΙΣΣΗΙΚΛΕΟΠΑΤΡΑΙ

ΤΗΙΑΔΕΛΦΗΙΚΑΙΒΑΣΙΛΙΣΣΗΙΚΛΕΟΠΑΤΡΑΙΤΗΙΓΥΝΑΙ

ΚΙΘΕΟΙΣΕΥΕΡΓΕΤΑΙΣΧΑΙΡΕΙΝΟΙΙΕΡΕΙΣΤΗΣΕΝΤΩΙΑ
ΒΑ

ΤΩΙΚΑΙΕΝΦΙΛΑΙΣΙΣΙΔΟΣΘΕΑΣΜΕΓΙΣΤΗΣΕΓΕΙΟΙΠΑΡ
ΕΠΙ

ΔΗΜΟΥΝΤΕΣΕΙΣΤΑΣΦΙΛΑΣΣΤΡΑΤΗΓΟΙΚΑΙΕΠΙΣΤΑΤ
ΑΙ

ΚΑΙΘΗΒΑΡΧΑΙΚΑΙΒΑΣΙΛΙΚΟΙΓΡΑΜΜΑΤΕΙΣΚΑΙΕΠΙΣ
ΤΑΤΑΙΦΥ

ΛΑΚΙΤΩΝΚΑΙΟΙΑΛΛΟΙΓΡΑΜΜΑΤΙΚΟΙΠΑΝΤΕΣΚΑΙΑ
ΙΑ

ΚΟΛΟΘΟΥΣΑΙΔΥΝΑΜΕΙΣΚΑΙΗΛΟΙΠΗΥΠΕΡΕΣΙΑΑΝΑ
ΓΚΑ

ΤΟΥΣΙΗΜΑΣΠΑΡΟΥΣΙΑΣΑΥΤΟΙΣΠΟΙΕΙΣΘΑΙΟΥΚΕΚΟ
ΝΤΑΣ

---

[1] Called also Ptolemy IX. [2] Wilkinson's *Egypt*, Murray, p. 408.

ΚΑΙΕΚΤΟΥΤΟΙΟΥΤΟΥΣΥΜΒΑΙΝΕΙΕΛΑΤΤΟΥΣΘΑΙΤΟΙ
ΕΡΟΝΚΑΙ

ΚΙΔΥΝΕΥΕΙΝΗΜΑΣΤΟΥΜΗΕΧΕΙΝΤΑΝΟΜΙΤΟΜΕΝΑ
ΠΡΟΣΤΑΣ

ΓΙΝΟΜΕΝΑΣΥΠΕΡΤΕΥΜΩΝΚΑΙΤΩΝΤΕΚΝΩΝΘΥΣΙΑΣ

ΚΑΙΣΠΟΝΔΑΣΔΕΟΜΕΘΥΜΩΝΘΕΩΝΜΕΓΙΣΤΩΝΕΑΝ

ΦΑΙΝΗΤΑΙΣΥΝΤΑΙΑΙΝΟΥΜΗΝΙΩΙΤΩΙΣΥΓΓΕΝΕΚΑΙΕ
ΠΙΣΤΟ

ΛΟΓΡΑΦΩΙΓΡΑΨΑΙΔΟΧΩΙΤΩΙΣΥΓΓΕΝΕΙΚΑΙΣΤΡΑΤΗΓ
ΩΙΤΗΣ

ΘΗΒΑΙΔΟΣΜΗΠΑΡΕΝΟΧΛΕΙΝΗΜΑΣΠΡΟΣΤΑΥΤΑΜΗ
ΔΑΛ

ΛΩΙΜΗΔΕΝΙΕΠΙΤΡΕΠΕΙΝΤΟΑΥΤΟΠΟΙΕΙΝΚΑΙΗΜΙΝ
ΔΙΔΟΝΑΙ

ΤΟΥΣΚΑΘΗΚΟΝΤΑΣΠΕΡΙΤΟΥΤΩΝΧΡΗΜΑΤΙΣΜΟΥΣΕ
ΝΟΙΣ

ΕΠΙΧΩΡΗΣΑΙΗΜΙΝΑΝΑΘΕΙΝΑΙΣΤΗΛΗΝΕΝΗΙΑΝΑΓ
ΡΑΨΟΜΕΝ

ΤΗΝΓΕΓΟΝΥΙΑΝΗΜΙΝΥΦΥΜΩΝΠΕΡΙΤΟΥΤΩΝΦΙΛΑΝ
ΘΡΩΠΙΑΝ

ΙΝΑΥΜΕΤΕΡΑΧΑΡΙΣΑΕΙΜΝΗΣΤΟΣΥΠΑΡΧΕΙΠΑΡΑΥΤ
ΗΙΕΙΣΤΟΝ

ΑΓΑΝΤΑΧΡΟΝΟΝΤΟΥΤΟΥΔΕΓΕΝΟΜΕΝΟΥΕΣΟΜΕΘΑ
ΚΑΙΕΝ

ΤΟΥΤΟΙΣΚΑΙΤΟΙΕΡΟΝΤΟΤΗΣΙΣΙΔΟΣΕΥΕΡΓΕΤΗΜΕΝ
ΟΙΕΥΤΕΧΕΙΤΕ

(Translation.)

LETTER OF THE PRIESTS TO THE KING.

"To king Ptolemy and queen Cleopatra his sister,
and queen Cleopatra his wife,
Gods Euergetæ, welfare, we, the priests of Isis,
The very great goddess (worshipped) in Abaton·
and Philæ,

Seeing that those who visit Philæ, generals, chiefs, governors of districts in the Thebaid,

Royal scribes, chiefs of police, and all other functionaries,

As well as their soldiers and other attendants,

Oblige us to provide for them during their stay,

The consequence of which is that the temple is impoverished,

And we run the risk of not having enough for the customary sacrifices and oblations

Offered for you and for your children.

Do therefore pray you, O great gods, if it seem right to you,

To order Numenius your cousin and secretary,

To write to Lochus your cousin, and governor of the Thebaid,

Not to disturb us in this manner, and not to allow any other person to do so,

And to give us authority to this effect, that we may put up a stele with an inscription

Commemorating your beneficence towards us on this occasion,

So that your gracious favour may be recorded for ever,

Which being done, we, and the temple of Isis,

Shall be indebted to you for this, among other favours.. Hail."

LETTER OF THE KING TO THE PRIESTS.

"To the priests of Isis in Abaton and Philæ, Numenius, cousin and secretary,

And priest of the god Alexander, and of the gods Soters, of the gods Adelphi,

Of the gods Euergetæ, of the gods Philopatores, of the gods Epiphanes, of the god Eupator,

Of the god Philometer, and the gods Euergetæ, greeting,

Of the letter written to Lochus,[1] the cousin and
    general,
We place the copy here below, and we give you the
    permission you ask
Of erecting a stele. Fare ye well. In the year
    .... of Panemus .... and of Pachons 26."

ORDER OF THE KING.

"King Ptolemy and queen Cleopatra the sister, and
    queen Cleopatra the wife, to Lochus our brother,
    greeting,
Of the petition addressed to us by the priests of
    Isis in Abaton and Philæ
We place a copy below, and you will do well to
    order that on no account they be molested
In those matters which they have declared to us
    Hail."[2]

THE OBELISK OF THE PIAZZA NAVONA.

To Domitian, the most stupidly cruel of all the
Cæsars, belongs the credit, if credit it be, of erecting
the next obelisk after the fall of the Ptolemies. This
obelisk is the one which is now most incongruously and
inconveniently placed on the rocks of the centre of
the Great Fountain in the Piazza Navona. It was
formerly believed by the archenthusiast Athanasius
Kircher[3] to have been one of the obelisks of Helio-

[1] All the preceding eight Ptolemies adored as deities, in accordance with
Egyptian custom. The junior members of the royal family were hereditary
priests and priestesses of the temples of these deceased monarchs, as many
of their funereal stele testify.

[2] A full description of this obelisk was published by W. J. Bankes, in
Geometrical plan of the Obelisk discovered at Philæ, London, 1824.

[3] Kircher was certainly a monument of erudition, and the author of a
great many most able, but most conjectural works. His *Œdipus Ægyptia-
cus*, and *Mundus Subterraneus*, are the chief; in the first of these he
attempted to unravel all the mysteries of the Egyptian language, and
even to write in the hieroglyphic script. Despite his wilful absurdities,
Egyptologists owe much to his memory as a reviver of ancient science and
forgotten traditions.

polis; but that idea is now proved to be wholly erroneous, inasmuch as the inscription is in honour of the Cæsar Domitian. The monolith is of red granite, and is about 54 ft. 3 in. high, by 4 ft. 5 in. at the base. It was discovered in the centre of the circus of Romulus and Maxentius, near the Via Appia, and in 1651 Pope Innocent X. employed the architect Bernni to restore and set it up again, since when discovered it was found to be broken into five pieces. Proud both of the obelisk and the commission, the fanciful architect could think of no better place to erect it in than on a mass of rock 40 ft. high, in the midst of the Grand Fountain in the Piazza Navona, and there it accordingly stands opposite to the Church of S. Agnese, and on the supposed site of her martyrdom ; an ancient monument on an artificial rock, with four fantastic figures representing the rivers of Europe, sitting over streams of water which issue beneath their feet. The obelisk having been erected by a member of the Pamphilian family, the obelisk was formerly called by that name also, but it has now resumed the topographical title properly belonging to it, and distinguishing it from the other obelisks of Rome. The inscription, according to Parker, but with some obviously necessary modification of the exact terms employed in his translation, reads thus :

" The Horus son of the sun,
  Sustainer of the worlds, giver of life to the worlds,
  The incarnate Horus, the son of the lady Isis,
  Who comes to avenge the death of his father Osiris,
  The king, living for ever."

These were only the usual epithet titles of the Pharaohnic kings, though they had a peculiarly inappropriate character as applied to Domitian.

The base of the obelisk is occupied by the following inscription in honour of Innocent X., and is

another example of the lengthiness of modern dedi-
catory inscriptions.'

South side.

INNOCENTIVS · X. PONT. MAX
NILOTICIS · AENIGMATIBVS · EXARA-
TVM LAPIDEM
AMNIBVS · SVBTERLABENTIBVS · IM-
POSVIT
VT SALVBREM
SPATIANTIBVS · AMOENITATEM
SITIENTIBVS · POTVM
MEDITANTIBVS · ESCAM
MAGNIFICE · LARGIRETVR

East side.

NOXIA · AEGYPTIORVM · MONSTRA
INNOCENS · PREMIT · COLVMBA
QVÆ · PACIS · OLEAM · GESTANS
ET · VIRTVTVM · LILIIS · REDIMITA
OBELISCVM · PRO · TROPHEO · SIBI
STATVENS
ROMÆ · TRIVMPHAT

West Side.

INNOCENTIVS · DECIMVS · PONT. MAX.
NATALI · DOMO · PAMPHILIA
OPERE · CVLTVQ · AMPLIFICATA
LIBERATAQ · INOPPORTVNIS · AEDI-
FICIIS
◆ AGONALI · AREA
FORVM · VRBIS · CELEBERRIMVM
MVLTIPLICI · MAIESTATIS · INCREMENTO
NOBILITAVIT

' Parker, *Roman Obelisks*, p. 8.

North side.

OBELISCVM
AB · IMP · ANT · CARACALLA · ROMAM
ADVECTVM
CVM · INTER . CIRCI · CASTRENSIS
RVDERA
CONFRACTVS · DIV · IACVISSET
INNOCENTIVS · DECIMVS · PONT. OPT.
MAX.
AD · FONTIS · FORIQ · ORNATVM
TRANSTVLIT · INSTAVRAVIT · EREXIT
ANNO · SAL M.DCLI · PONTIF VII.

On this occasion also a medal was struck, bearing upon one side a representation of the obelisk, with the legend, *Abluto aqua virgine agonalium cruore.*

OBELISK OF DOMITIAN AND TITUS AT BENEVENTO.

In the cathedral square of the ancient city of Benevento, there is a small and mutilated obelisk of red granite, the height of which at present is a little over 9 ft. ; it has several columns of hieroglyphics which do not appear to have been translated in detail. The general sense of the inscription is, however, to record the dedication and re-construction of a temple to the goddess Isis in Beneventum by the Emperor Domitian; and his cartouch, together with that of his coadjutor Titus, accordingly appears on the monument.[1] The title of Domitian runs thus : *Autocrator, Kaisaros, Domitianos Sebastos ;* and at the end of the column of hieroglyphics is the name of Lucilius Rufus, by whom the obelisk was probably set up.[2] It was certainly a strangely inconsistent conjugation to place together the names of Titus, "The Darling of Mankind," with that of the infamous

[1] Champollion Figeac, *L'Egypte,* p. 469.
[2] *Nestor l'hote,* No. I., p. 71.

Domitian upon the same obelisk, to record them as being both worshippers of the same benevolent god- dess, and as alike partaking of her divine nature. When the actors in such scenes have passed away, such inscriptions left behind become the imperishable pasquinades of history.[1]

OBELISK OF THE PASSEGGIATA, OR MONTE PINCIO.

The philosophical but sensual emperor Hadrian erected the obelisk which next demands attention, and the obelisk which bears his name, and that of his wife Sabina, was originally set up by him in honour and deification of his favourite Antinous, who had drowned himself in Egypt, in the Nile, with the idea of securing the happiness of the emperor in ac- cordance with the decree of an oracle, which had declared that the prosperity of Hadrian could only be obtained by the sacrifice of what was most dear to him; and whose death left the emperor incon- solable. To perpetuate the memory of Antinous, Hadrian founded a magnificent city in lower Egypt on the place of his death, and this obelisk was in all likelihood one of a couple which were erected there also, before the temple of Divus Antinous,[2] circa A.D. 131. Like all Roman works of that period it is small, being only 30 ft. high ; and the hieroglyphics are coarsely cut; there are two lines of hieroglyphics upon the face of the monument, and the apex is plain. So much of the inscription as has been read runs thus :

" The son of the sun,
 Lord of diadems,
 Hadrianus Kaisoros."

[1] There is a further fragment of the same obelisk in the wall of the Archepiscopal palace.
[2] An altar bearing the inscription ΑΝΤΙΝΟΩΙ ΕΠΙΦΑΝΕΙ, was discovered by the late Mr. Harris, during his excavations at Antinoe.

"The regent of the two lands,
Sabina,
Life, health, and strength,[1]
Sebaste,
Ever living."

Some years later the obelisk was removed from Egypt to Rome to beautify the Circus Varianus on Monte Pincio. In the fall of the Eternal City it shared the usual fate of all such monuments, and it lay concealed in the earth near the Church of Santa Croce in Gerusalemme till the year 1822, when Pope Pius VII. had it mounted upon a pedestal in the centre of the public promenade of the Passeggiata, from whence it is now generally called the obelisk della Passeggiata.

After the erection of this last obelisk no more inscribed obelisks were set up, either in Egypt or in Rome. For this there was ample reason; the Egyptian language had been entirely supplanted by the Latin and the Greek; the significance of the characters was unknown, already Pliny had proved his entire ignorance of the script, and Pliny it must be recollected was the learned centre of all the science of his time, by asserting of the hieroglyphics on the Obelisk of Thothmes III. in the Campus Martius, that they "interpreted the operations of nature according to the philosophy of the Egyptians;"[2] and a new school of thought had arisen, a school in which both Christianity and infidelity were factors; the school of thought which looked upon all these things with scorn, and placed the *summum bonum* ostensibly in philosophical humanity, but in truth in practical selfishness. All was decay hastened by furious

---

[1] This is the usual formula which succeeded the names of all the Egyptian kings, it was expressed by the following hieroglyphics ⚲𝌆𝍠.

[2] Pliny, *Hist. Nat.*, Book xxxv., Chap. 14.

passions and intense greed around them, and men
of science and men of war agreed but in one idea
of morality, the morality of existing in the present
and disregarding the future and the past alike.
The Edict of Theodosius, A.D. 379, formally closed
the temples of Rome and Egypt for ever; but
they had literally been long since neglected. Christianity, only just liberated from the thraldom of the
state, was voluntarily placing the world under the
worse tyranny of an ill-informed clergy, three fourths
of whom were infidels and heretics to the other
fourth, solely because the entire body had no settled
data to accept. In time all the excited ebullition of
faction wore itself out, the spirit of Christianity
prevailed, and left the letter to the employment of
scholiasts and mystics, when a new and more popular
system became prevalent in the world; the fresh
temples were places for general assemblage, in
accordance with the apostolic precept, " not forgetting
the assembling of yourselves together." ' A wholly
spiritual symbolism replaced the material and objec-
tive symbolism of Paganism; and, fit token of fit
change, the obelisk, perhaps the oldest of all religious
symbols, as it was the first to concentrate in itself the
adoration of the multitude to the sun, was the last to
be overthrown, when for Horus, Harmakhu, or Amen
Ra, rose in eternal glory another and a more perfect
" Sun of righteousness with healing in His wings."

THE ALBANI OBELISK.

This is a small obelisk, which was executed in Egypt
by Sixtus Rufus, who was prefect of that province, in
honour of one of the Roman emperors; for which purpose it was afterwards sent to Rome. The obelisk is
now at Munich; but further particulars concerning it
are not to hand.'

' Heb. x. 25.
' Westropp, *Hand-Book of Archæology*, First Edition, p. 56.

CHAPTER XXI.

Uninscribed Obelisks.

THE OBELISK OF THE VATICAN.

ONE of the loveliest scenes that Italian architecture affords, is rendered to the spectator
who stands on a summer day's decline in the Piazza
of St. Peter's. Before him rises, like a golden mountain robed in purple clouds, the massive dome of
St. Peter's, the glory of art and of Christianity. On
either side of the piazza sweep those long colonnades
which were the master conception of Bernini's mind;
in the middle, to the right, and the left, a rapid and
ample fountain casts up into the air its opalescent
spray; overhead depends the sevenfold arch of Iris;
and, central of all, fountain, piazza, and portico, rises
the lofty and yet slender Obelisk of St. Peter's, the
largest, most perfect, and best known of all the uninscribed obelisks in existence. 83 ft. high, by a
diameter of 8 ft. 10 in. at the base, it throws its long
shadow along the marble pavement, and glistens in
the rays of the setting sun, like the staff of a giant
crucifix before some ethereal shrine.

Owing to the entire absence of hieroglyphics upon
this obelisk, it is entirely a matter of conjecture by
whom it was originally set up, and consequently to
what dynasty it belongs. Pliny attributes its erection
to a monarch whom he calls "Nuncoreas, the son
of Sesores," and states that a still larger one, 100
cubits high, was made for the same monarch, which
he dedicated to the sun by the command of an
oracle, "after having lost his sight and recovered it;"[1]
this latter obelisk was, according to the Roman historian, still remaining in Egypt when he wrote. In

[1] Pliny, *Hist. Nat.*, Book xxxv., Chap. 15.

9*

this relation there is much that is improbable; the name of Nuncoreas does not occur in the Egyptian royal lists ; nine or ten other various readings have been suggested for it, Bunsen prefers to call the king, Menepthah I., the son and successor of Rameses II., but there is no indication in the annals of his reign of his ever having become blind. What is more certainly known is that the obelisk at first stood before one of the temples of Heliopolis, then that it was removed to Alexandria by Augustus, and subsequently transported to Rome by the emperor Caius Caligula. To convey this obelisk with greater safety, Caligula had a special vessel constructed to carry it, the length of which was nearly as long as the left side of the Port of Ostia, the sea port of Rome ; despite all this care it was broken in the carriage, and was the only one of the Egyptian obelisks which thus suffered in the transit to Rome.[1] When the monument was safely floated up the Tiber, the huge ship, or more properly galley, which had been designed to carry it was useless for any other purpose, and therefore, " after having been preserved for some years, and looked upon as the most wonderful construction ever beheld upon the seas, it was brought to Ostia, by order of the late emperor Claudius ; and towers of Puteolan earth being first erected upon it, it was sunk for the construction of the harbours which he was making there. And then besides, there was the necessity of constructing other vessels to carry these obelisks up the Tiber, by which it became practically ascertained, that the depth of water in that river is not less than that of the river Nilus." On arriving at Rome the obelisk was set up in the Spina of the Circus of Nero, a site now covered by the sacristy of St. Peter's, and it is the only monument of its kind which has been found in

[1] But according to the best authorities this obelisk is not broken, and if so, cannot be the one described by Pliny.

the place it was originally intended for, of course it has been removed to the situation which it now occupies. It was probably the circumstance of its being still perfect in the Pontificate of Sixtus V., which suggested to that Pontiff in 1586, the idea of raising up the other fallen obelisks which were known to underlie the surface of the city, and to remove this one from the ruins of the Circus to the square, or Piazza, of St. Peter's.

As nearly eleven hundred years had elapsed since such a vast monolith had been moved in Rome, the undertaking was one of considerable novelty and difficulty; failure was anticipated on all hands, and as many as five hundred plans were submitted to Sixtus V. by various engineers and architects who were desirous of trying their skill. At length the architect Domenic Fontana, who was already well known as a successful architect and mechanician, was selected by the Pope to transplant the obelisk ; an almost unlimited amount of labour was placed at his disposal, six hundred men, one hundred and forty horses, and forty six cranes, were engaged in the undertaking. A Pontifical celebration of High Mass, followed by the solemn blessing of Fontana and his workmen preceded the operations ; while the better to secure the engineer from officious molestation by the numerous spectators, it was declared an offence punishable with death for any one to speak during the operations. After all these precautions the undertaking had nearly failed at the last; owing to the extreme dryness of the weather, some of the principal ropes necessary to raise the obelisk, being new ones, became relaxed, and the utmost powers of the machines employed were unable to elevate the monolith properly in position. The silence of mortified pride and of baffled hope now took the place of the taciturnity imposed by fear, and it was nearly obvious to all, from the Pope to the humblest *lazzaroni*, and worst of all to the architect himself, that the attempt was a failure. At that most critical moment one of the workmen, a peasant named Bresca, conceived a method of increasing the tension of the cords; possibly he may have been a fisherman, at any rate, forgetting in his excitement the terrors of speech, he shouted out *Acqua alle funi*, "Wet the ropes;" quick to perceive the importance of the suggestion, Fontana instantly ordered water to be thrown over the tackle, and presently the ropes shrunk back, the levers creaked, and the massive obelisk was steadily elevated to its true centre, and the greatest engineering achievement since the Cæsars ruled in Rome was accomplished. Magnificent rewards were bestowed upon Fontana, half the value of the machines and materials; a sum amounting to 18,987 *scudi*, became his share. The workman Bresca, whose felicitous daring secured the success of the work at the risk of his own life, was also liberally compensated, and to his family was granted *in perpetua* the right of supplying palm leaves from Bordigheira, the home of the Bresci, for the use of the faithful on Palm Sunday, a concession which they still enjoy, and which has proved for three centuries a lucrative one.[1]

With much good taste Fontana when he re-erected this obelisk retained its original base, and although considerably obliterated by the decay of the stone, the following dedication of the monument by Caligula to his predecessors, Augustus and Tiberius, is still visible on two of its sides:

DIVO. CAES. DIVI. IVLII.	TI. CAESARI DIVI.
F. AVGVSTO	AVG. F.
	AVGVSTO SACRVM.

[1] Travellers' traditions ascribe the idea of wetting the ropes to the ingenuity of an English sailor, but the privileges still held by the Bresca family, for the services rendered by their ancestor on the occasion of the erection of the obelisk of the Vatican, places the matter beyond a doubt.

To these inscriptions Sixtus V. added as usual a longer one, viz.:—

SIXTO V. PONT. MAX. OPT. PRINC.
FELICI PERETTO DE MONTE ALTO PA.
PA. OB PVRGATAM PRAEDONIB. ITA-
LIAM RESTITVTAM INSTAVRATAMQ.
VRB. OBELISCVM CAES. E CIRCO NERON.
IN MEDIAM D. PETRI AREAM INCREDIB.
SVMPTV TRALAT. ET VERAE RELIGIONI
DEDICATVM S.P.Q.R. AD REI MEMOR.
OBELISC. HVNC P.

West side.

CHRISTVS VINCIT
CHRISTVS REGNAT
CHRISTVS IMPERAT
CHRISTVS AB OMNI MALO
PLEBEM SVAM DEFENDAT.

South side.

SIXTUS V PONT MAX
OBELISCVM VATICANVM DIIS GENTIVM
IMPIO CVLTV DICATVM
AD APOSTOLORVM LIMINA
OPEROSO LABORE TRANSTVLIT
AN. MDLXXXVI. PONT II.

East side.

ECCE CRVX DOMINI
FVGITE PARTES
ADVERSAE
VICIT LEO.
DE TRIBV IVDA

North side.

SIXTVS V PONT MAX
CRVCI INVICTÆ
OBELISCVM VATICANVM

AB IMPVRA SVPERSTITIONE
EXPIATVM IVSTIVS
ET FELICIVS CONSECRAVIT.
AN. MDLXXXVI PONT II.

On the summit of the Obelisk towards St. Peter's.

SANCTISSIMAE CRVCI
SIXTVS V. PONT MAX.
CONSECRAVIT.
E PRIORE SEDE AVVLSVM
ET CAESS AVGG. AC TIB.
I.L. ABLATVM M.D.LXXXVI.

The cross at the top was renewed in 1740, and a perforation made in it to receive some relics of our Lord.[1]

THE OBELISK OF ST. MARIA MAGGIORE.

This obelisk is one of a pair which, according to tradition, were set up at Memphis by king Pepi Merira of the VIth dynasty, a monarch who is recorded on the hieroglyphic texts to have reigned for one hundred years,[2] less one hour ; and who was one of the greatest as he was also the last Pharaoh of that dynasty. This tradition is, however, highly improbable, and all that is certainly known is that this obelisk and its companion one, now on Monte Cavallo, were removed from Egypt by Claudius Cæsar, A.D. 57, and placed by him at the entrance of the mausoleum of Augustus. When it was disinterred many centuries afterwards, it was found to have lost its apex, and to have been broken into three or four pieces. It is of red granite, and, without including its ornaments and base, stands

---

[1] The weight of the obelisk is about 360 tons, and its entire height, including the steps and cross, 132 ft. 2 in.

[2] This monarch was the Apappus of Eratosthenes. Manetho calls him Phiops, the monuments Pepi. He actually lived 106 years. Birch, *Rede Lecture.*

48 ft. 5 in. high, by 4 ft. 3 in. at the lowest diameter. Sixtus V., in whose Pontificate it was disinterred, employed the architect Fontana to re-erect it, and he caused the following inscription to be placed upon its pedestal :

SIXTVS V. PONT. MAX.
OBELISCVM
AEGYPTO ADVECTVM
AVGVSTO
IN EIVS MAVSOLEO
DICATVM
EVERSVM DEINDE ET
IN PLVRES CONFRACTVM
PARTES
IN VIA AD S ROCHVM
IACENTEM
IN PRISTINAM FACIEM
RESTITVTVM
SALVTIFERAE CRVCI
FELICIVS
HIC ERIGI IVSSIT AN. D.
M.D.LXXXVII. PONT. III.

On the other side.

CHRISTVS
PER INVICTAM
CRVCEM
POPVLO PACEM
PRAEBEAT
QVI
AVGVSTI PACI
IN PRAESEPE NASCI
VOLVIT

On the third side.

CHRISTVM DOMINVM
QVEM AVGVSTVS
DE VIRGINE

NASCITVRVM
VIVENS ADORAVIT
SEQ. DEINCEPS
DOMINVM
DICI VETVIT
ADORO

On the East side.

CHRISTI DEI
IN AETERNVM VIVENTIS
CVNABVLA
LAETISSIME COLO
QVI MORTVI
SEPVLCHRO AVGVSTI
TRISTIS
SERVIEBAM

THE OBELISK OF MONTE CAVALLO.

This obelisk is the companion of the preceding, and like it stood before the entrance to the mausoleum of Augustus. It was not unearthed till the Pontificate of Pius VI. in 1786. When discovered it was also found to be broken in several places, and to be without an apex. It is a little smaller than the obelisk of St. Maria Maggiore, inasmuch as it stands only 45 ft. in height, but it occupies a perhaps finer position than any of its companions in the city of Rome, except the obelisk of the Vatican, since the architect Antinori erected it on the place of the Monte Cavallo, between the two splendid bronze horses called Castor and Pollux, which once adorned the centre of the baths of Constantine, and are now the glory of Rome.

THE OBELISK OF ARLES.

This obelisk is a thick and rather heavy monolith of gray granite, 55 ft. 1 in. high, by 7 ft. 6 in. in diameter. It is very perfect, and is probably of Roman

workmanship, and was in all likelihood used as the
Meta of the Circus of Arles. It is evidently not of
Egyptian origin, since it is wrought out of the local
granite of the quarries of Mount Esterel, near Frejus.
It was found in the gardens of a private individual
near the walls of the city, which are but a short
distance from the Rhone. It had probably remained
here ever since it was landed, which must have been
near seventeen centuries ago, without ever having
been applied to the purpose for which it was intended.
It was quite buried in the ground, and only the point
was a little bare. We learn from the town archives
that Charles IX., circa A.D. 1389, when he was once
passing through the city, ordered the obelisk to be
dug out in order to be removed, but this was not done.
Afterwards the inhabitants of Arles raised it in
honour of Louis XIV. in one of the public places,
with pompous inscriptions on the four faces of its
pedestal. They have placed at its apex a globe
representing the earth, and above it a sun, which is a
real device (*une vraie devise*) without any inscription.[1]
Beneath the inscription in honour of Louis XVI. is
another referring to the late Emperor Napoleon III.[2]

OBELISK OF PHILÆ.

This is a small and rather more slender obelisk
than usual. It is wrought, not in granite, but in sandstone, and its apex is roughly broken off. According
to the measurements of Bonomi it is about 33 ft. high.

OBELISK OF FLORENCE.

In the Museum of Florence are two small obelisks,
which, however, are not a pair, as their dimensions
differ considerably, though their heights are nearly
equal. They are about 6 ft. high, in red granite, and

---

[1] Buchoz, *Correspondance d'Histoire Naturelle*, 1775, quoted by Zoega,
De usu et origine Obeliscorum, 1796.

[2] Murray's *France*, Ed. 1877.

with their pyramidion entire. They are the smallest obelisks in existence, and their history is unknown.

OBELISK OF CATANIA.

This is a Roman imitation, and is not a true obelisk, having eight sides. It formed the Meta of a circus, and had no religious significance attached to it.

There are, unquestionably, many other obelisks, inscribed and uninscribed, remaining underground beneath the modern buildings of Rome, Constantinople, and more especially Alexandria. Obelisks were not objects which could easily be used for building purposes, and the material of which they were made, a hard red granite, would not be useful to burn into lime, a fate which has befallen most of the smaller temples of Egypt.[1] Again obelisks when they fell down would require a considerable expense of time and skill before they could be re-erected, and, therefore, they were in the majority of instances allowed to lie where they fell, and then be covered over by subsequent elevations, since they were too heavy to be moved out of the way. Whether any more of these long hidden monoliths will be recovered is uncertain; but in the undisturbed *debris* of the Greco-Egyptian cities in the Delta, there must be still concealed many ruined works of art, and even many broken obelisks.

CHAPTER XXII.

THE OBELISK OF LONDON.

THE prostrate obelisk of Alexandria, now henceforward to be more honourably known as the

---

[1] See Gliddon, *Appeal to the Antiquaries of Europe*, 1841, on the destruction of the ancient temples under Mahomet Ali, for the sake of the lime in the stones of which they were composed.

Obelisk of London, is the westernmost of the two great obelisks, which, originally erected by Thothmes III. before the temple of Tum in Heliopolis, were afterwards removed by the architect Pontus, in the seventh year of Augustus Cæsar, to dignify the grand water entrances of the imperial temple or Cæsareum of Alexandria. Like its companion, when re-erected by the Romans, it was, instead of being imposed flat upon its pedestal, supported by four bronze claws or crabs, the oxidation of which has injured its surface, and eventually caused the overthrow of the monument; the obelisk having been upset to allow of the claws being wrenched away for the sake of the metal they contained. This overthrow must have taken place in comparatively recent centuries, for there is evidence that in the time of the Arab historian, Abd-el-lateef, both obelisks were standing, and were regarded as useful landmarks.[1] The obelisk is of red granite, and is 68 ft. 5½ in. long,[2] by about 8 ft. wide at the base; the apex is roughly cut and damaged, it having, like most of the obelisks of Thothmes III., been covered with a bronze cap. The base of the monument, and its two steps or gradines, remain entire; they are of limestone, and are nearly 7 ft. high. Owing to the position in which it fell, the monolith has been much exposed to injury, alike from the friction of the sand and the corrosive action of the salts in the sea breezes; indeed, the south side has suffered most of all, the hieroglyphics being in many places wholly illegible: the east face has also suffered severely : the west face, and that which rests upon the ground, has been better

[1] Abd-el-lateef (in his travels) expressly states that he saw two obelisks near the sea, without making any mention of one of them being on the ground; though when he speaks of the two obelisks of Heliopolis, he takes care to say that one of them had fallen. Qy., What has become of the fallen obelisk of Heliopolis?

[2] Or, according to Pliny, 42 cubits, or 63 ft.

preserved ;[1] but even Sir Gardner Wilkinson at one time decided that, as a work of art, the obelisk had suffered in too great a degree to render it worth while to remove it to London. Norden, who visited Alexandria, 1737, stated that the obelisk was also broken ; but that Messrs. Burton and Bonomi proved to be a mistake, when in 1827 they measured and published the two accessible faces of the monument in the *Excerpta Hieroglyphica*. After the visit of Bonomi, a house and also a part of one of the fortifications of Alexandria was built upon the obelisk,[2] and thus it seemed more improbable than ever that the monolith should be rescued from decay. The exposed portion served as a trial stone for every idle Greek or ignorant tourist to cut his initials upon ; and, from the broken angles of the base fragment by fragment was chipped away, to serve as a traveller's trophy to senseless admirers at home.

It seems not a little remarkable, considering the interest taken in the military successes of Great Britain by all classes of society, that an obelisk which would have most fittingly commemorated the battles of Alexandria and the Nile should not have been carried off by the victors in 1801, when they removed the Rosetta stone and several smaller antiquities. At that time indeed a vigorous effort was made by the General in command of the British army, to obtain the obelisk, and had not the zeal of General Lord Cavan been officially repressed, the trophy would have been long ago secured for the victors. A memorandum recently discovered in the Manuscript Department of the British Museum, gives so lively an account of the action taken upon this occasion that it is best to transcribe it nearly as it stands, since the circumstance has not been related by apparently any historian.[3]

---

[1] Long, *Egyptian Antiquities*, p. 302.
[2] Gadsby's *Wanderings*, Vol. I., p. 152. This was in 1852.
[3] *Athenæum*, No. 2604, Sep. 22, 1877.

"At the termination of the Campaign of 1801, in Egypt, M. General the Earl of Cavan was left in command of the portion of the British forces which was ordered to remain in that country, in which portion was included the Auxiliary Corps sent from India, under the command of M. General Baird.

"Lord Cavan soon turned his attention to the Obelisk denominated by us, 'Cleopatra's Needle,' which lay upon the ground, close to its own pedestal, and also close to another Obelisk of nearly the same dimensions, but not so perfect, which stood, and which it is understood still stands erect close to Alexandria, consequently close to the theatre of those wonderful achievements whereby Egypt was wrested from the dominion of Buonaparte, and restored to the Sublime Porte in that year.

"Lord Cavan conceived the notion of obtaining a grant of the fallen Needle for the purpose of conveying it to the Metropolis of the British Empire, there to be erected to commemorate the Victories of the British Arms in Egypt, under the Conduct of Sir Ralph Abercromby and Lord Hutchinson . . . . . Lord Cavan did, unquestionably obtain . . . . . a sufficient grant from the Turkish Authorities, and at once proceeded to carry his purpose into execution. Having conferred with our Chief Engineer on the spot, namely, Major Bryce, ... the plan for the embarkation and conveyance to England of the fallen 'Needle of Cleopatra' was prepared, and, upon due consideration, adopted.

"The troops then remaining in Egypt were invited by their Officers to subscribe a certain number of days' pay to meet the Expenses of an undertaking in which their feelings were deeply interested, an invitation which was eagerly accepted, so that Lord Cavan instantly found the necessary Funds for his purpose at his disposal. Officers, Non-Commissioned Officers, and Soldiers vied with each other in offering their

Contributions to the furtherance of an object so gratifying to their National and to their Professional pride, and the work was forthwith put in progress, in the following manner : One of the largest of the French Frigates (*El Corso*) captured at Alexandria was purchased, of the Prize Agents, from the Funds thus contributed, to convey the fallen Needle to England. A Stone Pier or Jetty was commenced, alongside of which, when completed, the Frigate was to be brought, to receive the Needle, which was to be introduced into the Ship upon Rollers, through a Stern Port to be cut to the necessary size, and when introduced was to be laid upon a Bed of large Blocks of Timber, forming a platform upon the Keel of the ship, so as to keep this immense weight of solid substance exactly a midship, and to prevent its straining the Keel. Thus placed in the hold of the Ship, the Needle was to be secured in its bed, so as to preclude the possibility of its being moved therefrom by the motion of the Ship at Sea. As the fallen Needle lay close to the Sea, the moving it upon Rollers from where it lay, to the Ship, became a very easy operation.

" Matters being thus arranged, the necessary Working Parties were alloted daily, in the general orders issued by M. Gen¹. the Earl of Cavan, and the undertaking proceeded most prosperously. To compensate the soldiery for the tear and wear of their Necessaries, Working Pay was issued to the Working Parties from the Funds to which they themselves had contributed.

" Considerable progress was made with the Jetty, and the Superior Officers of the Royal Navy then at Alexandria, viz⁺. Captains Larcom and Donelly, embarked most zealously and cordially in our project, which must therefore have been perfectly successful, had it not been abandoned, in consequence of orders received from Lord Keith, and General Fox, who at that time held the chief Command of the Fleet and of the Troops serving in the Mediterranean."

After some criticisms upon the causes which led to the abandonment of the projected work, the author of the manuscript continues thus : " The Working Parties were of course discontinued ; the bargain with the Prize Agents for the Ship was dissolved, and the Funds remaining undisbursed were returned to the Subscribers. The project of conveying the fallen Needle to England being no longer practicable, it was resolved that another expedient should be adopted, in order to establish some lasting Record of the results of so glorious an expedition ; accordingly, the uppermost Block of the Pedestal of the fallen Needle was raised upon one side sufficiently high, by means of levers, to admit of a space of about Eighteen Inches square being chiselled out of the middle of the lowest Block of the Pedestal.   In that space a brass plate was laid, on which was engraved a short detail of the principal Events of the Campaign."

The thirty years' peace turned the attention of the English from the affairs of Egypt, but in later years, every now and then, however, some zealous antiquary wrote to the papers an *ad-misericordiam* appeal on behalf of the obelisk of Alexandria, and then, for a brief time, a little correspondence was stirred up ; but it was generally felt that the removal of the obelisk was a national task, which ought to be undertaken by the Government ; and as the Government, whether Whig or Tory, never was of the like opinion, the discussion was always fated to fall through.   The chief obstacle was always the cost of the transport, which was generally estimated at £15,000, a sum too large to be granted for any single antiquity or work of art; the high prices which are now realized by the sale of paintings and porcelain being then unknown.   When, in 1831, Mahomet Ali offered the obelisk again to the

English, further proposing at the same time to defray
the cost of its removal to the ship or raft intended to
convey it to London, it was confidently expected that
his liberal present would have been accepted, and that
the more so, since the French, with better taste, were
already engaged in transporting the Obelisk of Luxor.
Motives of policy, and the fatal indifference of the
authorities to every ancient monument that was not
classic or mediæval, again repulsed the offer, and the
obelisk seemed finally .condemned to perpetual obscurity. Still, from time to time, questions were asked in
Parliament about the "Cleopatra's Needle," and opposition writers always found an allusion to its neglected
state a serviceable taunt against the ministry. Tired
of these constant attacks, the "present Government" of
1849 declared it was their intention to transport one
of the obelisks to the metropolis, and in the House of
Commons, April 15, gave as an estimate, "the height
of the obelisk, 64 ft.; its weight, 284 tons; and, as
before, the cost of carriage and removal, £15,000." [1]
Again public interest was excited in the matter,
various sites were mentioned, and their eligibility
freely canvassed ; but, after some further explanations
and delays, nothing was ultimately done; and the defence of the ministry was the opinion of Sir Gardner
Wilkinson, fortified by the addition of the opinions of
architects who only cared for classical antiquities:
" that the obelisk was too much defaced to be worth
removal." As an instance how even antiquarians may
sometimes justify government, Sir Gardner's words in
1858 are worth quoting. He is referring to the first
proposition of Mahomet Ali, to hand over the monument free of expense : " The project has been wisely
abandoned ; and cooler deliberation has pronounced
that, from its mutilated state, and the obliteration of
many of the hieroglyphics by exposure to the sea air,
it is unworthy the expense of removal." [2]

[1] Long, *Egyptian Antiquities*, p. 51.   [2] Murray's *Egypt*, p. 91.

In 1851, a year rendered memorable by the Exhibition of all Nations, the question was again brought before the House, and the proposition of removing the obelisk received the favourable support of Joseph Hume, perhaps the most conscientious economist that ever sat in the House of Commons. The expense was then estimated at £7,000 only, but again that outlay was deemed too great for its object; accordingly, the next advance was made in 1853, by the Directors of the Sydenham Crystal Palace Company, who, having decided upon building the beautiful courts representative of the architecture of various ancient nations, conceived the idea of planting the Alexandrian obelisk in the centre of the transept, near to the Egyptian court, which was then being completed by Bonomi. The thought was a happy and noble one, and the consent of the Government for the removal of the obelisk was formally applied for, and easily obtained. Once more expectation was aroused, and newspaper correspondence stirred up; the irrepressible "constant reader" plied the editor of his special "valuable paper," with numerous questions as to dynasties, monuments, and hieroglyphic writings; estimates were again prepared; and yet once again the design fell through, chiefly it is to be conjectured from the expense which would have been incurred by the transport of a monument, which, being national property, could only be lent to a private Company, and would hardly add to the dividends on the invested capital sufficiently to recoup the directors and shareholders for the intended outlay.

A few years later, namely, in 1867, "the subject of the removal of the obelisk was once more brought under the notice of the Government, in consequence of a notification from the Khedive, who had let the land on which it stood to a Greek merchant, and as he found that the obelisk was a tenant that paid no rent, he desired its

10*

absence; and in default of that buried it under the earth."[1] Like all the previous applications, however, even this of the Khedive himself produced no effect; and these constant failures proved to antiquaries, that if the obelisk were ever to be rescued from the sands of Egypt, it would have to be by the action of private munificence. Various distinguished literary men were appealed to; but literary men, though their pens convert their ink into liquid gold for òthers, rarely are able to obtain more of the *aurum potabile* than suffices for themselves. Certain antiquaries, who combine the artist and the pedlar, are sometimes more fortunate, but they rarely care to expend money on the preservation of anything which is not " their very own." More than once an attempt was made to start a Society to remove the obelisk by private subscription, and once more in 1876, and this time by General Alexander, who had partly cleared out the obelisk, and who had for seven years agitated by circular and otherwise for its removal. The Government was applied to for assistance, but then, as before, the Chancellor of the Exchequer declined to advise any grant in aid;[2] the ministry contented itself with promising to facilitate the removal of the obelisk by consular letters, and other inexpensive patronages, whenever the requisite amount of money was in hand; but that was all. Finally, last year Professor Erasmus Wilson, himself the son of an English sailor,[3] took the resolution of securing for London this interesting relic of Egypt's greatness and England's victories by sea and land, and engaged to undertake the whole cost of transport himself, the Government providing

---

[1] *Times*, February 12, 1877.

[2] General Alexander was informed that a Frenchman had threatened to remove the obelisk, and break it up; seven years did the General agitate the Government, the press, and his personal friends, but in vain. He estimated the cost of transit as only £3000 or £4000.

[3] Erasmus Wilson is the son of the late William Wilson, Surgeon, R.N.

a site for the monument when it should be landed.[1] The Board of Works agreed, that in the event of the obelisk being brought to London without cost to the Government, a site would be found for it on the Thames Embankment, wherever Mr. Wilson and his friends might afterwards decide; all risks and expenses were to be strictly borne by the donor of the obelisk. Fortified with that consent Mr. Wilson consulted an engineer, Mr. John Dixon, and he offered to remove the obelisk from Alexandria to London, and set it up again, bearing all risks, for a sum of £10,000. The contract was entered into on both parts, *con amore* as far as personal profits are concerned, and early in July Mr. Dixon arrived in Alexandria, where, not without having met with difficulties from the avarice of the natives, he soon unearthed and cleared out the obelisk, and to his great delight found it far less injured than had been anticipated. A tubular casing of iron 95 ft. long by 15 ft. diameter, was prepared to encase the obelisk which it was first proposed to protect from injury by nailing it up in thick planking, but no wood casing was required ; diaphragms were fixed around the shaft at regular distances, so as to form watertight compartments ; the iron plates were fastened to the circumference of these diaphragms, and so the cylinder was constructed.

When complete, the bank between it and the sea was removed, so that nothing but a moveable inclined plane lay between it and the waters ; wooden ways were laid to prevent the cylinder from touching the ground, and so the movement was commenced ; a rough bit of rock unfortunately pierced the casing, and the opening being under water, could not be got at, until the water was got rid of ; this caused a temporary delay, and then the rolling was resumed with success ; when she floated, the cylinder was towed

[1] See Appendix, *Wilson's Narrative.*

round to the western bay, and placed in the Khedive's dry dock ; and when repaired and fitted, was launched and started on September 21, 1877.

The following translation of the two faces[1] of the obelisk, those only which Burton was able to copy, is by M. Chabas :—

OBELISK OF LONDON.[2]

The inscriptions of this monolith are disposed exactly in the same order as those on the erect obelisk of Alexandria. The central column is by Thothmes III., and the two lateral ones from Rameses II. The copy was easier to obtain than that of the erect obelisk. Therefore the text is in a somewhat better state of preservation. But the side resting upon the ground was then invisible, and its inscriptions of course remained unknown.

Central Column (Thothmes III.), First Side.

" The kingly Horus,
Strong bull, crowned in Thebes,
The king of upper and lower Egypt,
Ra-men-Kheper,
He made (this) in his monuments to his father
    Horemakhou,
He erected two very great obelisks capped with gold
(When he celebrated) the panegyry of his father
    who loves him.[3]   He did (it)
The son of the sun,

---

[1] Also figured in Champollion le Jeune's *Monumens de l'Egypte.*
[2] From Burton's *Excerpta Hieroglyphica*, pl. 51.
[3] This passage is badly copied in Burton's work.

Thothmes, the best of existences,
Beloved of Horemakhou."

Second Side.

" The kingly Horus,
  Strong bull, ruling in truth,
  The king of upper and lower Egypt,
  Ra-men-Kheper.
  For him the Lord of gods has multiplied the
    panegyries[1] in Habennou,[2]
  Knowing that he is his son,
  The elder, the divine flesh,
  Issuing (from himself)
  To be . . . .[3]
  The son of the sun,
  Thothmes, Lord of Heliopolis,
  Beloved of Horemakhou."

Third Side.

" The kingly Horus,
  Strong bull, beloved of Ra,[4]
  The king of upper and lower Egypt,
  Ra-men-Kheper.
  His father Tum has established him, making for
    him a grandeur of name in expanded royalty,
    . . . . . in Heliopolis,
  (And) giving him the throne of Seb (and) the
    office of Kheper-Ra ;
  The son of the sun,

---

[1] Festivals of thirty years.   [2] The temple of the sun in Heliopolis.
              [3] The copy here is wrong.   [4] The sun.

Thothmes, the best of existences,
Beloved of the Bennou¹ of Heliopolis."

Inscriptions of Rameses II. in the right and left columns of each of the visible sides.

First Side I.

" The kingly Horus,
Strong bull, son of Tum,
The king of upper and lower Egypt,
Ra-ousor-ma-Sotep-en-Ra,
Lord of diadems,
Who protects Egypt
And chastises nations,
Son of the sun,
Rameses Meriamen,
Who throws down southern peoples
As far as the Indian Ocean
And the northern peoples
As far as the prop of the sky,
The Lord of the two lands,
Ra-ousor-ma-Sotep-en-Ra,
Son of the sun,
Rameses Meriamen,
Vivifier like the sun."

Second Side I.

" The kingly Horus,
Strong bull, beloved of Ma,²
The king of upper and lower Egypt,

¹ Sacred bird.   ² Truth.

Ra-ousor-ma-Sotep-en-Ra,
Lord of panegyries like his father Ptah Totanen,
Son of the sun,
Rameses Meriamen,
Strong bull, like the son of Ma,
None could stand (against him) in his time,
The Lord of the two lands,
Prenomen,
Son of the sun,
Cartouch: Rameses II."

Second Side.

1 "The kingly Horus,
Strong bull, son of Khepera,
The king of upper and lower Egypt,
Prenomen.
Golden hawk,
Of abundant years,
Very victorious,
Son of the sun,
Cartouch: Rameses II.
(He) enabled men to behold he has done,
Never was uttered denial (against it).
The Lord of the two lands,
Prenomen,
Son of the sun,
Cartouch: Rameses II.,
Splendour of the sun . . . .
2 The kingly Horus,
Strong bull, beloved of Truth,
The king of upper and lower Egypt,
Prenomen,

Son of the sun, offspring of the gods, possessor
of the two lands,
Son of the sun,
Cartouch: Rameses II.,
Who made his frontiers to the place he chose,
And got peace through his victory,
The Lord of the two lands,
Cartouch: Prenomen,
Son of the sun,
Cartouch: Rameses II.,
Splendour of the sun."

Third Side.

1 " The kingly Horus,
Strong bull, beloved of Ra,
The king of upper and lower Egypt,
Cartouch: Prenomen,
(Lord) of panegyries like his father Ptah,
Son of the sun,
Cartouch: Rameses II.,
Son of Tum, from his loins, who loves him ;
Hathor generated him ;
He who opened the two lands,
Lord of the two lands,
Prenomen,
Son of the sun,
Cartouch: Rameses II.,
Vivifier like the sun.
2 The kingly Horus,
Strong bull, son of . . .[1]
The king of upper and lower Egypt,

[1] Name undistinguishable.

Cartouch : Prenomen,
Lord of diadems, who cares for Egypt and
  chastises nations,
Son of the sun,
Cartouch : Rameses II."

Here the copy of Burton's *Excerpta* is wrong, and
the meaning of the passage is very doubtful. The
inscription was ended like the others, by the prenomen
and name of Rameses II.

APPENDIX TO CHAPTER XXII.

Cliff Field, Westgate-on-Sea,
Margate,

MY DEAR SIR,
        The only way by which I can meet your requirements is to set down, as Wilkie Collins says,

WILSON'S NARRATIVE.

In the autumn of 1876 I received a note from Sir James Alexander on professional matters, in which he referred to Cleopatra's Needle, which he was then busy in drawing attention to. As a sailor's son I took an interest in the matter; and on my return to London, having had a visit from Sir James, I was informed that a site for the obelisk had been awarded by the Metropolitan Board of Works on Sir James's solicitation; and that Mr. John Dixon, an engineer, had contemplated the means of effecting the object. A few days afterwards (we were then in November) I called upon Mr. Dixon, whom I had never seen before nor heard of, save through Sir James Alexander. Sir James Alexander had left him a few minutes before I entered. I soon found that Mr. Dixon was a Freemason, hence, all formality and ceremony were at once banished. He told me that he had long contemplated bringing the obelisk to England, and hoped some day to do it himself, when he should be rich enough ; he said that he and Mr. Fowler had talked over bringing it, but that political reasons had left the matter in abeyance. He then said, I should enclose the monolith in boiler plate, and roll it into the sea, I would then steady the cylinder by means of bilge plates, ballast it, fix a rudder, fix a cabin and spar deck, and then tow her to England. He said, he thought it might be done for £5,000, but he would enter into. a contract to do it for £7,000.

   *   *   *   *   *   *   *   *

Some further conversation took place, and Mr. Dixon was so confidant of his success, that we said this: "The undertaking is not an easy one; there may be unexpected difficulties, we *must* succeed; you say you can do it for £7,000, will you undertake to set it up safely on the banks of the Thames for £10,000; no cure no pay." "Willingly," was his answer, and we parted for the second time. "Mr. Dixon I have one more favour to ask of you, which is to give an interview to my friend, H. P. Stephenson, who is a civil engineer, and will influence us with his opinion; also a Freemason."

The following week, we four met at the solicitor's office in Bedford Row and agreed to the terms of a contract. Our next meeting was to sign that contract, in January.

Mr. Dixon then went to work in earnest, the cylinder was built on the banks of the Thames, and sent out in pieces. The rest you know.

A telegram of this day's date tells me that the *Olga* put into Algiers for coal yesterday, and at noon today started for Gibraltar.

Then we applied to Lord Derby for permission ; then we were told that that permission should be asked for from the Khedive, as England had refused the gift ; then obtaining the Khedive's assent in spite of previous refusal, we went upon the ground to take possession of the obelisk, but were stopped by M. Demetri, who said: "A short time back I wished to determine the property of the obelisk, and went to the courts demanding damages as rent from the Khedive ; the answer of the court was unsatisfactory: 'Do what you like with the obelisk, we have nothing to do with it;' and now, the man in whose interest this is said, gives authority to you to trespass on my land."

*   *   *   *   *   *   *   *

M. Demetri, however, in a true scientific spirit said, " I give the obelisk over to you Mr. Dixon, and those whom you represent; but I repudiate the authority of the Khedive."

Bisallah! What more shall I say ? Can you adapt your story to the thread which I now send you ?

The game then lies between Dixon and Wilson; the Government is out of the game altogether ; but we can't plant our baby on British ground without Government permission ; and, moreover, we expect Government to take care of it when it is so planted.

I suppose Parliament Square is out of the realm of the Metropolitan Board of Works, but the Metropolitan Board has not shown any backwardness in allowing us a site.   There can be no question as to the proper site, the best of all being Parliament Square ; there we should have a foundation of masonry and iron girders ; on the Thames Embankment, or in St. James's Park, we should have to make a foundation on piles.

Yours very faithfully,

ERASMUS WILSON.

P.S.   Tomorrow or next day I shall be able to send you a copy of my pamphlet, which is now in the printer's hands. In it you will find the special details you are in want of; but, as touching the obelisk, by-gones should be by-gones, and all recrimination wiped away. If you or I had been in the Government we should doubtless have acted as the Government has done, that is I hope so; but not being in the Government we needn't dictate to them what they ought to have done and didn't do.

* * * * * * * *

Let me know of anything that I can further explain.

E. W.

CHAPTER XXIII.

The Execution of the Obelisk.

PROSTRATE and half covered with sand, on the floor of the granite quarries of Syene, lies a stupendous obelisk, still partly attached to its native rock, and as perfect as on the day when the Egyptian miner took his chisel from its surface to finish his work another time; which other time has not come yet, though forty centuries have passed away since then. This obelisk, had it been completed, would have been one of the largest of its species, for it still measures 95 ft. long, by a diameter of 11 ft. 1 in.[1] At its side are yet to be seen the marks left by the wedges of the quarrymen of Pharaoh; and indications of the inclined road leading to the river can also be traced. From an examination of this obelisk, and of the walls of the quarry in which it was hewn, the method adopted by the Egyptians for severing such huge masses of stone from the rock becomes obvious ; and it was precisely the same principle as is now adopted by the natives of India, who have practised it from immemorial centuries. "The workman having found a portion of the rock sufficiently extensive, and situated near the edge of the part already quarried, lays bare the upper surface, and marks on it a line in the dircetion of the intended separation, along which a groove is cut with a chisel about a couple of inches in depth; above this groove a narrow line of fire is then kindled, and maintained till the rock below is thoroughly heated; immediately on which a line of men and women, each provided with a pot full of cold water, suddenly sweep off the ashes, and pour the water into the heated groove, when the rock at once splits with a clear fracture. Square blocks of

---

[1] Wilkinson's *Egypt*, p. 404; 11 ft. 1½ in., is the exact width.

6 ft. in the side, and upwards of 80 ft. in length, are sometimes detached by this method."[1]   This account agrees also with the statement of Agatharchides, that the rocks in the gold mines of Egypt were split by burning wood.[2]   In addition to the simple line of incision in the rock, the Egyptian masons used large wedges of soft wood, which they afterwards saturated with water, and thus rent the blocks asunder, carefully chiselling away at the same time, and in all probability using a large coarse saw to deepen the cuts.   When the mass of stone was nearly all cut through, the props which sustained it were knocked away, and it was allowed to break itself off from the rock by its own weight, a rather singular proceeding, as it risked the safety of the monolith.   There is no doubt, however, that that plan was adopted, since several of the large sarcophagi in the British Museum, as well as that of Seti I. in the Soane Museum, show where they have been sawn nearly through to the base, and then broken off.   In the Museum specimen the fracture has carried away a part of the basalt sarcophagus, and the hieroglyphics which run round its sides have only been slightly cut into the broken surface.   In the sarcophagus at the Soane Museum, on the other hand, the saw-break projects; and though the whole of the monument has been beautifully chiselled and polished, yet at the end the broken stone is allowed to protrude in all its original roughness.

When the obelisk was completely detached from the quarry, it was pushed upon rollers made of small palm stems to the water's edge.   There it was

[1] Sir J. F. Herschell's *Discourse*, quoted in Long's *Egyptians*, p. 304. He refers to the erection of a granite obelisk at Seringapatam. *Phil. Trans.*, IX., p. 312.

[2] These mines were situated in the Wady Ollaki; they were worked in all the greater dynasties of Egypt, and a series of interesting royal inscriptions, relating to the Pharaohs who visited them, is given in *Records of the Past*, Vol. VIII., p. 66.

surrounded with a casing of timber, and allowed to wait till the next inundation of the Nile conveyed it to the city where it was to be set up. Arrived at its destination the obelisk was once more propelled by rollers and levers up an inclined plane to the front of the temple where its base was already in position ; a firmer road of sand covered with planking was then made up to the very edge of the base and flush with its surface ; a deep and broad groove was next cut along the base, parallel to one of its sides, and parallel also to the edge of the base of the obelisk; the obelisk was next urged inwards till its lowermost edge rested in the groove on the pedestal ; long rollers, each thicker than the preceding, were then pushed by main force under the apex of the obelisk towards the base, till the monolith was gradually tilted upwards. Thus much achieved, strong date palm ropes were carried over the pylons of the temple in front of the obelisk, others were drawn round strong stays fixed in the ground, and by long-continued efforts, and the exertions of many hundred hands, the obelisk was at last lifted into position ; and it says much for the mechanical accuracy of the Egyptian masons, that so true was the level, both of the under surface of the obelisk and the top of the base, that none of the obelisks when erected were ever out of the perpendicular; a most important consideration, as owing to their great height and the narrowness of their foundations, a very small inequality would have sufficed to have overthrown them.

A point which must not be overlooked, was the rapidity with which, in some instances, the massive works were wrought and erected. The beautiful obelisks of Hatasu were quarried, set up, and covered with their hieroglyphic inscriptions within a space of seven months, an undertaking that, with all the modern resources of steam power and improved machinery, would almost be impossible to European

architects.[1]   There are no representations as yet discovered in the Egyptian bas-reliefs of the operation of
raising or removing an obelisk, though there is a well-
known one of the transport of a colossal statue.
Wheeled vehicles seem to have been very little used
for the carriage of great weights, a kind of sledge or
slip having been used instead.   The pulley of the
Egyptians was also a simple one, and there is no
indication of the knowledge of a compound lever.
Yet with all these imperfections they never seem to
have failed in any of their undertakings ; probably, or
indeed most certainly, a devotional spirit, such as is
the life of all true art, sustained and directed them in
their enterprizes.   One anecdote relating to the erection of an obelisk has been preserved by Pliny, but
the' extravagance of his details prevents any credence
being attached to his relation; and the action of the
monarch in the impending failure of the engineers is
utterly antagonistic to Egyptian thought or Egyptian
manners. . The Roman historian, starting as usual
with an imaginary chronology, thus narrates :

" Rameses, too,[2] who was reigning at the time of
the   capture   of   Troy,   erected   one   (an   obelisk)
140 cubits high.   Having quitted the spot where
the palace of Mnevis[3] stood, this monarch erected
another obelisk, 120 cubits in height, but of prodigious
thickness, the sides being no less than 11 cubits in
breadth.   It is said that 120,000 men were employed
upon this work ;[4] and that the king, when it was on

[1] Birch's *Egypt*, p. 86.
[2] This must be meant for Rameses III., who came into contact with
some of the Pelasgic peoples.   See also Gladstone's *Homeric Synchronisms*,
for a series of clever conjectures as to the Egyptian prince Memnon of Homer.
[3] Qy., the palace temple of the bull god Mnevis or Ba-en-Tattu, "The
Spirit that is in Tattu," the abode of Osiris, at Memphis.
[4] "This," Hardouin says, "was the same obelisk that was afterwards
erected by Constantius, son of Constantine the Great, in the Circus Maximus at Rome, whence it was removed by Pope Sixtus V., in the year 1588,
to the Basilica of the Lateran."   Note to Bohn's *Pliny*.

11*

the point of being elevated, being apprehensive that the machinery employed might not prove strong enough for the weight, with the view of increasing the peril that might be entailed by due want of precaution on the part of the workmen, had his own son fastened to the summit, in order that the safety of the prince at the same time might ensure the safety of the mass of stone. It was in his admiration of this work, that, when king Cambyses took the city by storm, and the conflagration had already reached the very foot of the obelisk, he ordered the fire to be extinguished; he entertaining a respect for this stupendous erection which he had not entertained for the city itself."[1]

When the obelisk was once placed in position, the labours of the sculptor and workmen were not over, for a scaffold had next to be erected, to enable the engraver to cut the hieroglyphic inscriptions, a work of considerable nicety and difficulty; for the characters of the hieroglyphics in good Egyptian work were never crowded or confused, a due systematisation of space was always preserved; and, the better to effect this purpose, one hieroglyph was substituted for another of a similar phonetic or syllabic value, to avoid confusion or defect. No allowance was made for optical perspective, since the characters were of the same size all the way up; indeed, those of the apex, containing a separate text, were generally in a smaller size, as were also the dedicating lines at the bottom of the monument; and from summit to base every portion of the obelisk was carefully sculptured and highly polished. Nothing was left unfinished; and with such precision and truth were the laudatory sentences inscribed upon the rigid stone, that neither the mallet of the Persians, the fire of the Romans, the salt sand of the desert, or the corrosive rains of the equinox, have been able to efface, or even to disfigure them.

---

[1] Pliny, *Nat. Hist.*, Book xxxvi., Chap. 14.

Such were the Egyptian obelisks, unique, grand, and symbolical, which devotion reared upwards to the sun ere any of the empires of the West had emerged from obscurity. They were ancient at the foundation of Nineveh; their history had become lost in the clouds of mythology, long ere the erection of the walls of Rome; to Solomon's Egyptian bride they must have been ancestral monuments; to Pythagoras and Solon, records of a traditional past antecedent to all recollection. Before the obelisk of Usirtesen, Potipherah the priest of On must often have bowed, attended by his slave-boy Joseph; and from the nunneries[1] which were gathered round it, and whose ruins still lie hidden underground, that slave-boy, then a rising minister, took his Egyptian wife. In the college to which that obelisk was attached, Moses, the meekest of all men, learnt the wisdom of the Egyptians. When, after the terrible last tenth plague, the mixed multitude were driven forth from Egypt, the light of the pillar of fire threw the shadow of that obelisk across the path of the fugitives. Centuries later, when the wrecked empire of Judæa was dispersed, it was again in the precincts of the obelisk of On that the exiled people of the Lord took shelter. Thither were carried some of those translators of the Holy Scriptures, who, at the command of Ptolemy Philadelphus, transcribed the Septuagint. Last of all, it was to the village of Matarieh, still in view of the obelisk of Usirtesen, that the infant

[1] Every Egyptian temple had, what might be called its nunnery, where young women of good family were educated by the wives of the higher clergy, and were taught to serve in the temple of the divinity, not exactly as priestesses, but as assistants. *Ahi-t* was the Egyptian term for them. They must not be confounded with the Pallakists, or wives of the gods; for these women could, and indeed generally did, marry out of the temple boundaries, and were very probably perfectly chaste. They were simply dedicated to the divinity, as in Catholic countries many young children are dedicated to the B. V. M., and wear a peculiar dress, without any ultimate intention of taking the veil.

Jesus was carried in the arms of his mother, in obedience to the command of the angel in a dream, "Arise, and take the young child and his mother, and flee into Egypt, and be thou there until I bring thee word."[1] Upon how many scenes has not that obelisk looked? Amidst how many changes of dynasty has it not held itself erect? Admired, if not worshipped, honoured, if alone, still it stands, where Usirtesen placed it four thousand years ago, the oldest and most typical of all the obelisks of Egypt.

[1] Matt. ii. 13.